why moths hate thomas edison

why moths hate thomas edison

and other urgent **inquiries** into the **odd** nature of **nature**

Edited by Hampton Sides

Illustrations by Jason Schneider

The Best of *Outside* Magazine's "The Wild File"

W. W. Norton & Company   New York London

The present work appeared in a slightly different version in *Outside* Magazine.
The publisher gratefully acknowledges Elizabeth Royte and
Patrick Clinton for permission to reprint their work.

For information about permission to reproduce selections from this book,
write to Permissions, W. W. Norton & Company, Inc., 500 Fifth Avenue,
New York, NY 10110

The text of this book is composed in Sabon
with the display set in Tarzana Narrow
Composition by Gina Webster
Manufacturing by Haddon Craftsmen
Illustrations by Jason Schneider
Book design by Chris Welch

Library of Congress Cataloging-in-Publication Data

Why moths hate Thomas Edison and other urgent inquiries into the odd
nature of nature : the best of Outside magazine's "The wild file" / edited by
Hampton Sides.
p. cm.
ISBN 0-393-32150-9 (pbk.)
1. Natural history—Miscellanea. 2. Nature—Miscellanea. I. Sides, Hampton. II. Outside magazine.
QH45.5 .W48 2001
508–dc21   2001016266

W. W. Norton & Company, Inc., 500 Fifth Avenue, New York, N.Y. 10110
www.wwnorton.com

W. W. Norton & Company Ltd., Castle House, 75/76 Wells Street,
London W1T 3QT

3 4 5 6 7 8 9 0

contents

FILE 3/ worldlywise

FILE 4/ up there

FILE 5/ further life forms

the feral circus

W hen I came to work at *Outside* back in 1993, one of my first projects was to develop and edit a new question-and-answer column for the magazine. Focusing on natural science and outdoor lore, the column would range widely, from the gothic to the comic to the cosmic. The idea was to solicit the sorts of questions about the strange doings of the natural world that most of us stopped asking (at least out loud) when we were eight years old. Idle questions, stupid questions, rogue questions. Insistent questions that arrive unexpectedly in daydreams or in elevators or in the shower. Questions that emanate from natural history's prodigious dustbin of myths, canards, and bald-faced lies. Questions we're supposed to know the answers to but don't and probably never did.

Why are the oceans salty? Why are there so many worms writhing on sidewalks after a storm? Are beavers ever flattened by the trees they gnaw down? What good are goosebumps? Is the earth leaking anything into outer space?

Getting readers to come up with these sorts of questions, we imagined, wouldn't be difficult once we had them thinking in a certain way. Befuddlement over the natural world is the human condition. Or rather, it's the kid condition. But somewhere along the way to adulthood, for reasons that aren't entirely clear, we seem to suppress the question mark.

So that was our first task, to recapture the unrestrained bemusement of youth. When kids want to know something, they just ask. They're unselfconscious about sounding dumb. When an answer doesn't satisfy, they ask again, and again. They can tell when we don't know, and they keep at it until they pin us to the wall. That sort of relentless curiosity seemed like just the right temperament for a column that would concern itself with mysteries like oceans, woods, bugs, stars, and snow.

Mainly, though, we wanted "The Wild File" to be fun to read. David Quammen, the eminent science writer who is a long-time contributor to *Outside,* once said that a great nature column should be "equal parts science and vaudeville." That's a formula we took to heart. We proceeded with the assumption that the natural world is an endlessly entertaining spectacle to be marveled at—a freakshow, a trapeze act, a tractor pull. At the same time, we embraced the corollary assumption that rather than being removed from the natural world, we humans are in every sense performers in the feral circus. In other words, the column would proceed from the premise that people are wild animals too, that our behaviors and physiques, our foibles and design flaws, are simply further oddities to be viewed under nature's Big Top.

New magazine columns are experiments. One never knows whether the material will take hold with readers and last. We were unsure whether the readers would join in the spirit of things, steadily sending in the inspired questions that would be the column's lifeblood.

Well they did. Soon after "The Wild File" debuted in the November 1994 issue with the question, "How high do birds fly?" the trickle of reader mail swelled into a steady stream that shows no signs of abating. *Outside* now receives, on average, one good question every day, via mail or e-mail, or through the on-line version of the magazine (*www.outsideonline.com*). Seven years and nearly 100 columns later, "The Wild File" has consistently been one of the magazine's most popular departments. So it is to you, the column's loyal followers and correspondents, that we owe our greatest appreciation. You're our co-conspirators. This book wouldn't be possible without you, sick and deranged though some of you may be. Week in and week out, you dared to dignify odd and sometimes idiotic-seeming thoughts by turning them into interrogatives. And then you went one step further—you affixed your name to them for public consumption. Thank you.

But someone has to *answer* the questions. Who is this all-seeing, pocket-protector-wearing Oz figure? Actually, that "person" has been several different people over the years. Patrick Clinton, a suffer-no-fools polymath and beloved professor then at Northwestern University's Medill School of Journalism, was the column's original writer. In 1996, the mantle was turned over to the very funny and gifted natural science writer, Elizabeth Royte. When Elizabeth took off for the jungles of Panama to research a book on field biologists, I stepped up to the plate. Although "The Wild File" continues to grace the pages of *Outside,* this book represents the work, in roughly equal proportions, of the column's first three writers.

People often want to know how we come up with the answers. That's easy. We started by creating something called the Wild File Bunker. It's a vast complex set deep in a salt cavern in the remote mountains of northern New Mexico. The Wild File Bunker is a place where answers are taken very seriously. There are digital clocks set to Greenwich Mean Time, banks of computers winking in climate controlled rooms, and lab-smocked technicians sipping smart drinks while tracking various research projects by Palm Pilot.

Ask a question and chances are pretty good the answer can be found somewhere in the dust-free corridors of The Bunker. If not, then we take a slightly more old-fashioned research approach: We get on the phone and find someone who knows the answer. As Patrick, Elizabeth, and I discovered, one of the real joys of writing "The Wild File" was the telephone sleuthing. We often had to go down decidedly odd paths to find experts in a number of extremely arcane fields. You could say that we specialized in locating specialists. Or rather sub-specialists—the sub-ber the better. We found to our endless delight that there was no topic too abstruse or absurd to have been studied, and studied at tremendous and sometimes neurotic lengths. Someone out there has pondered for years, perhaps whole lifetimes, nearly every stray question that might cross the threshold of our whimsy. Finding these various eminences and gurus was often tricky, but they were out there: People who study snowflakes, ball lightening, and the biochemistry of "gamy" meat. Experts on camelid biology, elephant psychology, leech behavior. Bee people, tornado people, moss people. A magnificent illustration of this came in August of 1996 when a reader wanted to know why "lizards are always doing push-ups." To field this irresistible question, Patrick Clinton figured he'd track down a good general-interest herpetologist and be done with it, but he soon found he could do much better. Somehow Patrick located a woman who had clocked 150 research hours observing and analyzing some 1,600 "calisthenic incidents" in the wild for her Ph.D thesis. Lizard excercise was her medium. "She made my day," says Clinton, "and I think I made hers."

Among the many wonderful things we learned from the experts is that every feature and phenomenon of natural science, no matter how esoteric, has a name. For example, the odd twitches that humans (and many other animals) display when they're drifting off to sleep are officially known as "hypnic jerks." When llamas really feel like ruining your day, the foul green slime they come up with is called "visceral spit." That uncontrollable urge to sneeze in bright light? "Photic sneeze reflex." Thanks to experts who dream up this stuff, everything has a name. And in the naming, the strange and incomprehensible already seem somehow less formidable.

In most cases the experts were thrilled to learn that someone beyond their field's narrow corridors cares even a smidgen about what they do. They rarely patronized, even though we gave them ample opportunity to do so. They're busy, busy people, but they took the time to explain. For the most part, their answers were cogent, good-humored, and inspired. So it is to you, Doctor Foremost in Your Field, that we owe our second giant debt of gratitude. This book couldn't have come into being without your cooperation—and forbearance. As Elizabeth Royte put it, "They deserve a medal for tolerating our benightedness and our incorrigible habit of scratching at inane points."

The delightful wrinkle in all of this, however, is that even the experts can't answer the questions all of the time. Either that, or they disagree on the answer so fundamentally that it's clear science hasn't figured it out yet. Sometimes they come right out and admit it, and other times they dance around the topic until the kid in us finally pins them to the wall. They may know exactly why the sky is blue, but they still don't know why dogs roll in dead animal carcasses. To me, it's deeply comforting that despite the painstaking efforts of all the scientists and naturalists out there, we still only have a superficial clue about how the natural world really works. Often even the most eloquent explanation isn't so much an answer as it is a window to another question.

This is a good thing. We should rejoice in our ignorance. The universe is still an enchanted place, even for know-it-alls. We came into this life asking, and if we're lucky, our inquisitiveness will never be sated. It's the happy alpha and omega of this world: In the beginning, there was a question. And also in the end.

Hampton Sides
Santa Fe, New Mexico
October, 2000

There are a number of people whom I must now shove out onto the stage for a special bow beneath the klieg lights, whether or not they want the attention: John Barstow, the fine editor at W. W. Norton who astutely shepherded this project from beginning to end; the three gifted artists who illustrated "The Wild File" during the initial years—Steve Yang, Brian Rea, and Jason Schneider (who also illustrated this book); Larry Burke, *Outside*'s ever-enthusiastic publisher; editor Mark Bryant, under whose tenure the column was conceived and launched. *Outside*'s current editor, Hal Espen, who expanded and fine-tuned the column; Katie Arnold for keenly and patiently editing my own pages; Dianna Delling, for invaluable editorial assistance; Eileen Rhine, for crucial technical support in pulling together all the old columns from the archives; Link Sides, Dorothy Wilkerson, and Walker Wilkerson, for their careful eyes; and last but cer-

The feral circus

13

tainly not least, the many crack researchers from the Wild File Bunker who labored in obscurity (not to mention poverty) nailing wispy clouds to the hard cold bulletin board of Fact. A special thanks to you all: Michael Behar, Emily Sandoval, Brooke DeNisco, Alex Wells, Chris Dray, Lia Mehos, Lorien Warner, Lolly Merrell, Michael Kessler, Tara Munkatchy, Willow Older, Jenny Ford, Tyler Stableford, Laura Slavik, Julie Moyers, Cristina Opdahl, Claire Martin, Eva Dienel, Anna Milkowski, Tasha Eichenseher, Heidi Schwindt, Danica Tutush, Lea Aschkenas, Kimberly Lisagor, Will Rizzo, Gillian Ashley, Jake Brooks, Grant Davis, Eric Hansen, Nate Hoogeveen, Mary Catherine O'Connor, Jane Maguire, Peter McDonnell, Jill Davis, Marc Peruzzi, Joe McCannon, Marc Peruzzi, Danielle Wolffe, and Christian Nardi.

Finally, please know that "The Wild File" proudly lives on in the pages of *Outside*. Currently the column is in the very capable hands of writer Stephanie Gregory, a former editor and long-time friend of the magazine. As always, we want, we need, we *must have* your questions! Send them to Outside, 400 Market Street, Santa Fe, New Mexico 87501, or submit them via Outside Online (on the World Wide Web at *www.outsidemag.com*). Your answers will be forthcoming.

why moths hate thomas edison

14

life forms

faunal knowledge

Farces of nature from the animal kingdom

Q Do beavers ever get squashed by the trees they're gnawing down?

—*Lauren Griggs, Syracuse, New York*

A All the the time. "I don't recall having seen one myself," says North Carolina State University wildlife researcher Richard Lancia, "but it is known to happen—and I have seen pictures." The beaver's reputation as a canny woodsman appears to be a bit overrated. "People think beavers can cut trees and know exactly where they're going to fall," says Lancia. "The fact is, they have no idea what's going to happen." Sure, they can be fairly accurate at dropping timber for their dams, but by the water's edge they usually have gravity on their side: trees right along rivers and lakes already tend to lean toward the light and open space. Get beavers away from the shore, however, and they can be downright inept. Sometimes, in thick woods, a beaver will gnaw through the bark of a tree that simply won't fall, because the surrounding branches are holding it up. This creates consternation for the beaver while stirring immense merriment in the beaver-research establishment. "They'll go in and cut it again, and again, and again," says University of Massachusetts biologist Joseph Larson. "But the tree is still standing!"

Q Do opossums really play possum?

—Edgar Smythe, Atlanta, Georgia

A Grab an average specimen of *Didelphis virginian* by the tail, and chances are it will assume a characteristic pose: back curled, eyes blank, fingers clutching. Just to make your life more interesting, it will also defecate, drool copiously, and release a green, foul-smelling liquid from its anal glands. Our catatonic marsupial, however, is not just pretending: It's really and truly *out cold*. "You can freely handle them, and even touch one of their eyeballs, and there's no reflex whatsoever," explains Alfred L. Gardner, curator of mammals for the National Biological Survey. "The animal doesn't respond to pain."

The odd thing is, most opossums won't pass out until they're actually caught, at which point common sense would say it's way too late to play dead. So why do they do it? It might be because many predators draw out the act of killing (think of a cat playing with a mouse before eating it), a habit that might protect them from consuming diseased prey. It's possible that when the opossum goes limp, the predator simply loses interest, thinking that not only is this potential entrée dead, it's *bad* and dead—that is, sickly, infected, or otherwise "off." Gardner has come across a good number of chewed and mutilated (but nonetheless living) opossums in his day, which he says suggests that playing possum really does work.

Except sometimes, as Gardner recently learned when called to consult on a criminal case involving a certain restaurant worker who'd been arrested for torturing an opossum. The reporting police officers were sure that the creature's neck had been broken, as it just lay there with its eyes wide open, drooling. "When it woke up," Gardner reports, "it looked at them and passed out again." A classic case, except for the ending: To put the animal out of what appeared to be its misery, the cops tenderly placed it beneath a tire of their patrol car and drove over it. Which goes to show that nature can arm you against your enemies, but when you come up against someone who wants to do you a favor, you're on your own.

Q How do deer run so quickly through dense woods without poking out their eyes on branches?

—*T. Mascarich, Clifton, New Jersey*

A "I've never encountered a blind deer," says eminent Canadian deer researcher Valerius Geist of the University of Calgary, "even though many can run nearly fifty miles per hour." There are several reasons why those big, orblike eyes go unscathed. For one, bucks and does don't make a habit of wandering through alien forests, hewing instead to well-trod trails in familiar necks of the woods. As in the famous *New Yorker* cartoon, deer tend to see the world as a circumscribed geography, and they come to memorize every tiny obstacle in their territory. Moreover, deer, being naturally frugal with their energy, rarely run at all unless spooked by a predator. Mainly, though, they're able to avoid blinding arboreal pokes and thwacks because they're equipped with thick, hardy eyelids and lightning reflexes. "Deer are far superior to humans at detecting minute changes in their environment and then performing precise reactions in a limited time frame," explains Geist. "Among bow hunters, there are well-documented stories of deer spotting arrows in midflight and then blithely sidestepping them. So a little tree branch is not going to pose a problem."

Q Why do llamas spit?

—Leo Patterson, Arlington, Virginia

A Llama sputum comes in two flavors: mild and vile. The mild stuff is simply whitish saliva, and these sociable herd animals use it as a medium of discourse. Because they have powerful lips and ample supplies of spit, llamas, like their cousins the vicuñas, alpacas, and guanocoes, evolved this curiously fluid communication system to convey many of the mundane signals of everyday life—to enforce herd hierarchy, to reprimand the young, to shoo off overeager lovers. Now for the vile stuff: When llamas get *really* upset about something, or when they're clearly threatened by a predator (or an aggressive tourist), they can let loose with a hot green slime the camelid experts call *visceral spit*. It comes from way down in the *rumen,* or the first compartment of the stomach, and it's memorably foul. "It's a stinky, sour mash of bacteria, digestive juices, and fermented grass," explains Virginia veterinarian Donna Matthews. "It can really ruin your day." Thankfully, llamas are slow to anger, and they'll usually alert you to an imminent outburst by pinning back their ears, craning their necks, and pointing their noses to the sky as their vexation rises, with the gastric juices slowly pooling in their mouths. "Some of them are Olympic-caliber spitters that can hurl a pint of the stuff up to fifteen feet away," notes Ohio State University veterinary professor David Anderson. "But then they hold their mouth open in shock, as though embarrassed to have done something so disgusting."

Q Are elephants really afraid of mice?

—Stephanie Locke, Honolulu, Hawaii

A It makes no intuitive sense that a six-ton beast should be frightened by a creature that weighs only a couple of ounces, but, in fact, elephants do shy away from various members of the order *Rodentia*. It's not quite the way you see it pictured in cartoons, however, with an otherwise proud pachyderm recoiling in atavistic dread at an ancient nemesis. Because elephants have crummy vision, and because they generally prefer life at a languid pace, they can't abide sudden surprises or jerky movements in their lumbering midst. Not only do elephants have trouble focusing at close range, but, with their eyes set on the sides of their enormous heads instead of facing forward, it's hard for them to get a good clear bead on anything that's small and jittery darting around beneath them. "In the wild, a large herbivore with no natural predators doesn't *need* to have good eyesight," explains Alan Roocroft, an elephant specialist affiliated with the San Diego Zoo. "In the open expanses of the bush their poor vision poses no real problems for them, but when elephants are kept in the confined quarters of captivity—in circus barns and zoo stalls—it's not uncommon for them to have close encounters with mice, and it just drives them nuts." They pull up their trunks, thrash their heads about trying to find a better sight line, and eventually

life forms

22

commence stomping the mystery object—at which point you can bet it's the mouse that's running scared.

Q Why do dogs roll in really gross stuff?

—Burt Ailes, Waterford, Virginia

A Dog researchers are divided on the purpose of this endearing trait. Whatever it is, it appears to be a lupine thing. Just like dogs, wolves are known to slap on such heady fragrances as urine, vomit, feces, and eau de rotting squirrel carcass. Some experts suggest that dogs and wolves do this to be more "at one" with their territory. Others suggest that our annoying canids are trying to mask their own scent for hunting, or trying to repel certain insects. Maybe they're trying to leave their own chemical Kilroy in the mess for the benefit of other sniffers. Another theory suggests, oddly enough, that it's a *social* trait. "Studies show that dogs are bringing back information about their turf," says Pat Goodmann, an Indiana wolf expert who actually wrote her master's thesis on this subject. "They're telling the pack what they've found, helping to develop mental maps of the area." Which is all well and good, except that with domesticated dogs, "the pack" is you.

But there's a more obvious explanation, notes Mark Derr, a well-known Miami-based canine authority: "Dogs do it because they actually *enjoy* the smell. They're like those people who can't walk past the perfume counter without spraying the stuff all over themselves."

Faunal knowledge

23

Q How *do* porcupines make love?
—Franklin Gerard, Reno, Nevada

A Actually, it's easier than you might think. After a courtship ritual that involves a fair amount of what in kinkier human circles might be called "water sports," the female simply folds her tail over her back, creating a quill-free platform for the male to rest on. The mating process is repeated until one of the porcupines abruptly breaks away, climbs a tree, and then—for reasons that aren't entirely clear—shrieks abuse at the other. It's not a pretty sight, all in all, but it doesn't seem to be painful.

Q Is polar bear liver really the most poisonous substance on Earth?
—Susan Magee, Tiffin, Ohio

A No, but if for some reason you're tempted by *pâté arctique,* be advised that as little as a mouthful can cause abdominal pain, headache, nausea, dizziness, and a torpor that lasts for days. A couple of ounces can make your skin peel off or even kill you.

Westerners have known this since 1596, when the Dutch explorer Willem Barents and his party nearly perished after eating the stewed liver of an Alaskan *Ursus maritimus.* The Eskimo have known even longer. For centuries they've buried polar bear liver to keep their dogs from getting into it. But it wasn't until the 1940s that two British biochemists identified the toxic ingredient: vitamin A. Polar bears live atop a food chain that's extremely high in vitamin A, and they can tolerate levels that would kill most animals. The excess is stored in their liver.

Drinking alcohol, by the way, can intensify the effects of a vitamin A overdose. Keep this in mind: friends shouldn't let friends eat polar bear liver drunk.

Q What are those weird antennas on top of a giraffe's head?

—Greg Hayward, Toronto, Ontario

A Those aren't antennae, they're skin-covered horns. Both males and females sport them, but they have no positively proven purpose—though it's possible that they serve as cooling towers. "The horns are heavily vascular, with an open bone structure," says large-mammal specialist John Lehnhardt. "They may provide a heat-dispersal opportunity." The male's horns come into play during sparring sessions, but they do no damage—sort of like jousting with a pair of carrots.

Q How long does it take a skunk to reload?

—David Stanley, Flint, Michigan

A Skunks store their noxious spray in two glands the size of Ping-Pong balls. They can squirt the stuff over and over again in rapid-fire sequence, letting fly with as little as a teaspoon or as much as half a cup. "Skunks can form a sort of U and 'look' at you with both ends at once, firing with bull's-eye accuracy," notes University of New Mexico mammalogist Jerry Dragoo. Theoretically, the skunk will eventually run out of spray if he gets angry enough, but in practice it never seems to happen. Dragoo, who was once sprayed by a single skunk eight times in one torturous minute, puts it this way: "I've yet to come across an empty gland."

Q What is it that pushes lemmings over the edge?
—Joe Marotta, Steubenville, Ohio

A Yes, the legendary mass plunges of the lemmings—all those sad, misguided rodents hurling themselves off the cliffs. Is it pack behavior run amok? Is it some kind of self-sacrifice for the sake of the species? Or is it, as some have theorized, the lemmings' effort to return to their ancestral home in Atlantis?

If you're like many Americans, the image of the lemmings' group belly flop was burned into your brain by the Disney film *White Wilderness*. But Disney got some of the key details wrong. In fact, the lemming-suicide thing is a myth that was started long ago, most likely in Scandinavia. Like their cousins the voles, lemmings have a boom-and-bust population cycle. When a boom gets really out of hand, lemmings swarm out of the hills, presumably in search of less populated territory. Some undoubtedly tumble into the fjords from time to time, but it must be stressed that these deaths are *accidental.* After such migrations, people began to notice that there were no more lemmings around, and this gave rise to the speculation that they must snuff themselves en masse.

The weird thing is, although lemmings don't commit suicide, they do commit murder on a fairly big scale: Current research shows that lemmings respond to overcrowding with infanticide and other Caligula-like frenzies of intraspecies violence. Being a nice family-values outfit and all, Disney didn't really want to get into that.

Q Why are polar bears so mean?

—Dave Cooper, Bermuda

A Although it's true that the largest land carnivore on Earth has been known to dine on the occasional stray *Homo sapiens,* polar bears don't hold any personal grudges against us. Unlike other bruins, these fierce arctic roamers stay active in the winter and thus must consume enormous amounts of high-calorie seal blubber—they can ingest as much as 10 percent of their body weight in half an hour—to keep their half-ton mass fueled in the frigid temperatures. Because there's not much action on the monochromatic ice pack, they're programmed to treat every movement as a sign of a potential meal. So if you happen to pop up on their horizon, chances are they'll investigate. This is not a pleasant scenario: they can sprint at twenty-five miles an hour and have a rather gruesome habit of delicately chewing on the heads of their victims before breaking out the fine china and getting down to business. Although polar bears do consume the occasional human, the numbers really don't add up to very much. Fewer than ten people have been killed by polar bears in the past thirty years.

Q Do camels exist anywhere in the wild?

—Clyde Cowan, New York, New York

A Yes, but sadly they appear to be headed the way of, well, *Joe* Camel. The genus *Camelus* originated in North America forty million years ago, give or take a few weeks. It was a smallish animal then, about the size of a hare, and humpless. Over time, some took the land bridge to Asia; others moseyed down to South America, where they evolved into guanacos, vicuñas, alpacas, and llamas. For unknown reasons, the North American prototype became extinct ten thousand years ago. Today, as a result of its usefulness to humans, the one-humped (dromedary) camel survives only in domesticated form. But in the Gobi Desert of Mongolia and western China, about one thousand two-humped (Bactrian) camels still live in the wild. They're endangered, though, mostly because humans are constantly taming them. It's easy to understand why. With shorter legs and thicker hair than their Arabian counterparts, Bactrians are valuable beasts—the Toyota trucks of the Gobi—capable of hauling up to a thousand pounds of people, cargo, and Chinese takeout.

that's fowl!

Q How high can birds fly?
—Anthony Segovia, Austin, Texas

A On November 29, 1973, over Abidjan, Ivory Coast, the voyage of a large bird was interrupted by a commercial jet at thirty-seven thousand feet. The bird's remains—five complete feathers, fifteen partials—were later identified as belonging to a Rüppell's griffon, *Gyps rueppellii,* a vulture.

Too heavy to rely on wing flapping alone, big scavengers are unrivaled masters of riding updrafts. Some African vultures have been observed making trips of sixty miles—and barely moving their wings after takeoff. "But that's not flying," you might sneer. "That's *soaring.*" Such sticklers would then give the record to thirty swans spotted by a pilot at twenty-seven thousand feet over the Outer Hebrides in 1967. Next in line is a mallard that smashed into an airplane at twenty-one thousand feet over Nevada in 1962.

As it turns out, the griffon record might have been a case of neither flying nor soaring. British ornithologist Colin Pennycuick, who has studied African vultures from a motorized glider, suspects that the griffon was sucked up in a violent thunderstorm—a real hazard in West Africa. "If so," Pennycuick says, "it would probably have been frozen solid by the time the airliner clobbered it." All the same, we're sticking with the unlucky vulture. Whether he was a visionary or just a frozen ball of feathers tossed in the path of destiny, he still got there. Effort is admirable, but elevation is . . . well, it's elevating.

Q Why do pigeons constantly bob their heads?

—Sam Derwin, Hanover, New Hampshire

A Head bobbing is a common trait among ground birds like pigeons, pheasants, partridges, and chickens. Ornithologists call it the *optokinetic response,* and it seems to help the birds' vision. Remember that a pigeon's eyes are set on the sides of its head, so that when it's walking around, the world sort of sails by in a confusing blur, like landscape viewed from a fast-moving train.

The optokinetic response appears to compensate for

this. Next time you're down at St. Mark's Plaza, take a look. The pigeon has a kind of inchworm gait. It jerks its head forward, then brings its body to meet it, then jerks its head forward again. The net result: The bird gets a series of fixed snapshot images, rather than a long, continuous blurry one. (A twirling ballerina uses a similar strategy, keeping her head aimed at a fixed point as long as possible while her body rotates.)

Back in the late seventies, Barrie J. Frost, a visual neuroscientist at Queens University in Kingston, Ontario, put pigeons on a tiny treadmill. They walked, but they didn't move relative to their environment, and they stopped bobbing—scientific proof, in case you needed any, that if you're going to get anywhere, you have to stick your neck out.

Q If you took a rooster up to the land of the midnight sun, would it crow?

—*Clay Wass, Denver, Colorado*

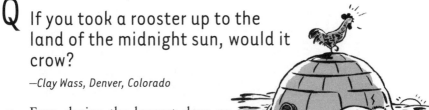

A Even during the longest days up above the Arctic Circle, you still get a slight nocturnal dimming. And roosters can be set off by the subtlest of dawns. So yes, in all likelihood, our hypothetical great northern cock will crow. Which of course begs the question—why do roosters crow in the first place? It has nothing to do with circadian rhythms or some burning barnyard mission to announce the new day. (Let a rooster out after he's been locked in a closet for ten minutes, and he'll crow just as loudly.) Paul Siegel, a poultry behaviorist at Virginia Tech, says morning crowing is strictly a turf thing. It's as if the rooster were warning, "Now that we can all see again, just remember—this stuff is *mine!*" In any case, you can forget Chaucer's brave Chanticleer: Nature's alarm clock is just another insecure male trying to scare off the competition. It's a wonder anyone gets up in the morning.

Q I've heard that eagles mate in midair and sometimes die when they fall to the ground during the act. Is this true?

—Ronak Harshad Shah, San Luis Obispo, California

A It is true that eagles will occasionally lock talons and plummet earthward, and some books on the subject have described this as part of their courtship dance. But love's got nothing to do with it. Says Montana State University eagle authority Al Harmata: "When one eagle swoops down a thousand feet, grabs another's talons, and then they try to knock each other out of the sky, that's not courting. That's fighting."

In fact, eagles can't mate on the wing, because the male, like the male of most bird species, doesn't have a penis. Instead, both male and female eagles come outfitted with more discreet forms of reproductive plumbing known as *cloacae,* which make avian mating more like a carefully

life forms

aligned kiss. It's tough enough for impassioned eagles to get all their ducts in a row without lift, yaw, and air turbulence.

Q How do they get goose down? Is it a poultry-processing by-product, or are living birds subjected to unspeakable torture?

—Rebekah Creshkoff, New York, New York

A No, you won't find concentration camps full of naked, shivering geese behind the L.L. Bean plant. Most down comes from slaughterhouses—Chinese slaughterhouses, to be exact, thanks largely to the Asian taste for waterfowl. Of the roughly 7.1 million pounds of down and feathers imported into the United States in 1995, about 6.4 million pounds came from China, Hong Kong, and Taiwan. If you were thinking of warming yourself with more humane alternatives this winter, consider this: feathers and down represent some 20 percent of the value of a goose, so if you switch to a synthetic, the doomed goose will still end up in someone's pot and a poor farmer will suffer.

Down *can* be harvested by more humane means, however. In Iceland, home of the endangered eider duck, down collectors climb cliffs and "defeather" old nests in a labor-intensive process whose cost, of course, is passed along to the consumer: eiderdown runs more than $300 per pound. There's also "hand-plucked down," another expensive product coming mostly from Europe, that's gathered by massaging the breasts of live geese. This procedure causes the birds mild distress, but compared to the gruesome destiny of millions of other geese in Europe—foie gras—it seems an infinitely kinder fate.

Q How do penguins keep their feet from freezing?

—Mitch Schieffer, Austin, Texas

A Although Antarctic penguins routinely stand around in thirty-below weather, their vulnerable-looking feet are padded with fatty tissue and protected by thick, leathery skin that— on the chilliest of days—keeps them a relatively toasty thirty-three degrees. That's still pretty cold, but it's not a problem for penguins, partly because some of the muscles that operate the feet are located up inside their warm, blubbery bodies. One other neat trick: By rocking back on their heels and tails, they reduce the pedal surface area that comes in direct contact with the ice. A klutzy-looking survival strategy, to be sure, but hey—whatever works.

Q How do ducks float?

—Louis Hall, Shawnee, Kansas

A Waterfowl have all sorts of nifty adaptations that help them stay afloat. To wit: Their bones and quills are hollow, they have buoyancy sacs inside their bodies, and their thick down traps air pockets all around them. But the real key to duck flotation is oil. Ducks and other waterfowl come equipped with little onboard grease factories called *uropygial glands,* located on the tops of their tails, which produce an oily substance composed of wax and fat. When you see a duck preening in the water, it's actually engaged in a maintenance session critical to its survival. The duck reaches back to scoop up a bill-full of uropygial oil and then liberally coats its feathers with the gunk, thus waterproofing itself.

But if oil is the duck's big secret, why is petroleum oil just about the worst thing a duck can run into? "Petroleum breaks down the natural oils," explains Scott Stephens, a waterfowl biologist with Ducks Unlimited. "It's too heavy and viscous. It mats the feathers together so they can't hold air." And when that happens, the oil-slicked bird sinks like a stone.

Q Do scarecrows really work?
—Trevor Anderson, Oklahoma City, Oklahoma

A Not very well, and not for very long. "Birds aren't stupid," says Cornell ornithologist Kevin J. McGowan. "If the same object doesn't move for weeks, they'll eventually figure out that it's not dangerous." For a scarecrow to work, it needs three things: fairly constant motion, realism, and daily variety of placement—which perhaps explains why you'll sometimes see starlings roosting on those stationary (and patently fake) plastic horned owls. Today you rarely spot scarecrows of the old-fashioned variety, because people finally got wise to the fact that they just don't work. Instead, farmers have adopted more radical methods, such as periodically blasting carbide cannons, setting up high-frequency electronic signals, and rigging their fields with inflatable mannequins that suddenly pop up like gunslingers in an arcade game. In Japan, farmers have been experimenting with enormous "scary eye" balloons that scowl ominously over rice paddies. All of these techniques have been only marginally successful, however. But there is one technique that seems to be gaining increasing interest: In recent years farmers have been erecting large stereo speakers in their fields and orchards and playing continuous loop tapes of the distress calls of the target bird—a blackbird, say, or a starling. The flock, hearing what sounds like one of their own being killed and eaten, stays away. The real breakthrough, McGowan argues, will occur when we enter the age of the Robocrow. "The only perfect scarecrow is going to be an android," he says, noting that his proposal for an animatronic owl has yet to be picked up by scarecrow R&D. "It'll take a while."

Q Why do geese fly in V formation?
—Dorothy Samson, McLean, Virginia

A The international goose research establishment has been investigating this one for quite a while. Some ornithologists speculate that much like fighter jets that fly in V-shaped squadrons, migrating geese might simply have found that the wedge is the easiest way to keep an eye on one another; that is, there are no "blind spots." We also know that, if it's done right, flying in formation can save energy. A goose that positions itself correctly in the updraft of another's vortex can hitch a free ride—saving, by some estimates, up to two-thirds of the power needed to keep it aloft. To conserve that much, however, the birds have to fly in just the right position— each goose trailing the one in front of it by about two feet, with wing tips slightly overlap- ping—and they rarely manage this degree of precision. So although they are saving energy, they aren't saving nearly as much as they could.

$V_+ \text{VELOCITY} = time^2$

$V - \text{FORMATION}$

GOOD!!!

FORMATION # 3

NO!

Q Do ostriches really bury their head in the sand to avoid being attacked?

—Roberta Hopper, Seattle, Washington

A Chickens are not cowardly. Hyenas don't really laugh. And no, the world's biggest birds do not plunge their heads below ground when confronted with a strange or difficult situation. In fact, quite the opposite: No practitioners of avoidance behavior, ostriches, which are native to the semiarid grasslands of eastern Africa, are extremely jealous and scrappy micromanagers of their turf. They're hypervigilant, with keen, bulging eyes that are actually larger than their brain. (Hey, no one said they were smart.) Where, then, did this famous canard come from? Well, ostriches do *eat* sand to provide grist needed for their gizzard, so their beak is often caked with the stuff. And when they're resting, they tend to droop their neck and lay their head down on the ground. Try balancing your noggin all day long on what is essentially a three-foot-long rubber band, and you'd do the same. Ostriches also tend to droop their head during thunderstorms, in what is believed by some experts to be a kind of atavistic electrocution avoidance technique. It's thought by some that the whole head-burying myth might owe its origin, in part, to a simple optical illusion: If you spot a clump of resting ostriches from a distance, their prostrate heads appear to be lost, or "buried," in the swimming waves of the heat shimmer. They're not avoiding you, however. As soon as they detect your presence, they'll pop up their heads and, if provoked, they'll charge you with their muscular legs and menacing two-toed feet. You've become their reality; they're dealing with it.

biodivertissement

Kinks and links in the great chain of life

Q What is the world's largest organism?

—*Isabel Garner, Monte Rio, California*

A Let's begin with the weakest among the oft-cited contenders to the throne: Australia's Great Barrier Reef. Promoters of Aussie tourism have brazenly lobbied for the GBR for years, pointing out that it extends for one hundred thousand square miles and supports more than sixteen thousand species. This is all well and good, but it's beside the point. Anyone who's ever put on a snorkel and a pair of fins will instantly dismiss a reef from consideration because it is a *community* of organisms, not a single one. So let's move on from pretenders to legitimate claimants: Whale lovers will exalt the great blue, undoubtedly the largest animal on Earth, with an average adult length of about ninety feet and a weight of more than 150 tons. But don't talk about blue whales to the folks over at California's Sequoia National Park. "The blue whale isn't even close to our General Sherman tree," insists a spokeswoman for the park. At last count, the General was 275 feet tall, and its trunk had a volume of 52,500 cubic feet—room enough to fit eleven blue whales. Sadly, General Sherman's supremacy took a hit in the midseventies, when mycologists isolated a colony of *Armillaria ostoyae,* a common fungus, whose millions of interconnecting tendrils extend over 1,500 acres in Klickitat County, Washington. This jumbo fungus enjoyed the title until 1992, when a group of biologists announced that a 106-acre stand of aspens in Utah was actually forty-seven thousand trees connected by a single root system. In terms of area, the fungus still rules; in terms of mass, the aspen grove has both the fungus and the giant sequoia beat. General Sherman has been duly demoted from "largest living thing" to "largest living tree." The Australian Tourist Board, however, has yet to amend its Web page.

Q How and when are organisms considered members of the same species?

—Orvin Bontrager, Aurora, Nebraska

A The traditional answer to this question is the one we learned in high school: If two organisms can mate and produce fertile offspring, then they're members of the same species. Most of us were taught that varieties within a species (say, two different kinds of ground squirrels) can always reproduce, but an organism cannot leap across the great divide and successfully mate beyond their kith and kin. A tiger and a lion can mate, but the resulting *liger* is, like a mule, sterile.

So far, so good. The problem is, this old-fashioned, reproductively based definition of what constitutes a species is full of holes. The natural world affords us endless examples that blur or outright violate this tidy conceptual paradigm. Take, for example, the race-runner lizards of the American Southwest, which reproduce *parthenogenically*— that is, the females clone themselves without any need for males whatsoever. Or for that matter, any of the thousands of plants and organisms, like blue-green algae, that reproduce unisexually. Then, too, there are many varieties of birds and fish that are known to mate successfully outside their own species—outside their own genus, even. "Ducks are especially promiscuous," notes Northwestern University's David L. Hull, a specialist on the philosophy of evolutionary biology. "They seem to get a little bored with their own species and blithely ignore the boundaries we've set for them." The fact is, although common sense tells us that the old concept works in most cases, professional taxonomists have long since stopped using it as the crucial criterion for defining a species. Today's classifiers, who like to call themselves *phylogenetic systematists,* have come a long, long way from the musty days of Audubon and Linnaeus. Steeped in Darwinian theory and armed with powerful computers that analyze the DNA strands of sample plants and animals, modern taxonomists are less interested in who's mating with whom, and more impressed by what they call *evolutionary lineages*—that is, which ancestor did the species evolve from, and how is it related to other species, both living and extinct, in the great family tree of biological diversity? Scientists today study an organism's genetic makeup and look for all sorts of esoteric connections, or *clusters*. It's on the basis of these minute determinations that new species are declared and the great scorecard of Earth's life is kept up-to-date.

Q I left the gas on in my kitchen, and the smell was just like skunk. Is that possible?

—*Emily Kerwin, Forest Hills, New York*

A Pure natural gas has no odor, which is a major drawback from the perspective of safety, so gas companies add what they call an *odorant*. The most common odorants are *thiols*, compounds that are present in lots of bad-smelling things, from sewage to rotten eggs. And yes, thiols are the same chemicals that make skunk spray so unforgettably rank. The big difference, according to chemical ecologist William Wood of California's Humboldt State University, is that the gas company tends to use thiols that are gaseous at room temperature, whereas Pepé Le Pew favors thiols that remain in liquid form. The smells, at any rate, are quite similar. "I'd classify them both as mephitic," says Wood. *Mephitic,* by the way, derives from *mephitis,* which Webster defines as "pestilential or foul exhalation from the earth" and which also is the name of the genus to which skunks belong. Case closed.

Q Why is it that an animal's eyes seem to glow when struck by light, while a human's don't?

—*Steven Rubin, Baltimore, Maryland*

A Our eyes *do* reflect light, as all flash photographers know—they just don't do it very well. The distinctive "eyeshine" given off by wolves and raccoons and crocodiles, among many other species, comes from the *tapetum lucidum,* a mirrorlike layer of cells in or behind the retina. This structure is found mostly in nocturnal animals, for whom it serves as a kind of light amplifier. The retina captures some of the light that enters the eye, but some passes through. The tapetum lucidum bounces it back at the retina, giving the animal a second chance to "see" it. It's this ricocheting light that gives off the vaguely eerie glow we've come to associate with macabre children's tales—all those sinister pairs of eyes staring out from gloomy thickets. So why don't humans have this advantageous after-hours adaptation? Probably because we evolved as diurnal creatures in the sunny, hot climes of the African savanna, where too much light, rather than too little, was our special obstacle to overcome. Anyway, because the tapetum lucidum lies behind the retina, the light it reflects is slightly out of focus. Maybe you'd be willing to sacrifice a little visual clarity in exchange for better night vision; our species apparently wasn't.

Q Why does scat stink? You'd think it would draw predators—an evolutionary disadvantage.

—Turner Ryan, Denver, Colorado

A Sure, ripe droppings can let a predator know that prey is in the neighborhood. But don't forget that smell works both ways: Herbivores, for instance, are extremely sensitive to the sulfur compounds present in carnivore droppings. If a deer happens to stumble across some fresh wolf spoor, it might rethink the day's foraging plans.

The predator-prey thing, however, is an incidental issue here, for scat stench serves a far more important role in the wild. When it comes to communication, animals do it with dung. Scat is an almost universal mode of discourse among animals of the same species, transmitting information about territory, feeding strategy, and the like. "Most mammals other than people are far more inclined to use chemical cues to communicate than other kinds of displays," says Russ Mason of the Philadelphia-based Monell Chemical Senses Center, a kind of think tank of smell.

Consider your dog on its morning walk. When it pauses

to examine another dog's calling card, it's involved in a fairly detailed act of social intercourse, learning what competitors or eligible mates have been around, what's been on the menu—important stuff. It's as if it's reading the newspaper. Had the scat been scentless, your dog might have missed it altogether. And, really, what good is an uninformed pet?

Q I hear that scientists have decided that mushrooms are animals. Am I missing something?

—*Nicholas Fox, Chicago, Illinois*

A In 1993, a team of molecular biologists tried to construct an evolutionary family tree of all living organisms by analyzing ribosomal RNA. The study revealed something surprising: Fungi and animals shared a common branch. On the great tree of life, in other words, mushrooms turned out to be our brothers, whereas plants are only our cousins. "There is some organism that lived a billion years ago that was the common ancestor of all animals and all fungi," says biologist Mitchell Sogins, one of the study's authors. Go back even further and we find the ancestor of that organism and plants. Go back even further and, as Sogins puts it, "everybody's unicellular."

The similarities between animals and fungi are striking enough that some scientists study human neurology by examining yeasts. And it's believed that one of the reasons that many fungal skin diseases are so hard to treat is that, on the molecular level, they resemble human tissue. Maybe it's time to start thinking of athlete's foot not as an infection, but just another relative who won't leave.

Q Am I imagining this, or is garbage sometimes warm to the touch?

—Reginald Lane, Charleston, West Virginia

A No, you're not imagining it. What you're feeling is the heat generated by millions of fast-replicating microbes as they gorge themselves on the organic matter contained in your trash. Spores of bacteria and microscopic fungi are out there perpetually blowing around in a dormant state, but once they land in a nice, dank pile of garbage, whether it be an outdoor compost heap or simply a kitchen trash can, they immediately go to work colonizing the stuff. Rubbish, you might say, is their medium. And as their numbers inexorably grow, so does the collective body heat. The responsible party here is aerobic bacteria, so as long as the refuse heap in question is well ventilated, it's going to generate warmth. Compost piles can reach temperatures as high as 180 degrees F, at which point the bacteria start to bake to death in their own metabolic stew, and the temperature levels off. Although garbage heat can be successfully harnessed—groovy Whole Earthers have done experiments in which they've heated water by coursing pipes through active compost

life forms

piles—unfortunately the Btu output is not consequential enough to turn heads at Texaco. But what about huge urban landfills? "Landfills, being oxygenless environments, don't produce heat but they do produce awful-smelling sulfides and steady seepages of methane that can be collected and sold to power companies," says Texas garbage consultant Bill Carter. "In some places, the methane builds up so fast that wells must be drilled deep into the landfill to keep it from blowing up."

Q What is that "gamy" flavor you sometimes taste in wild meats?
—*Eli Haber, Somerville, Massachusetts*

A *Gamy* is an all-purpose adjective we use to describe the strong, earthy essence of certain rustic meats like venison, duck, and wild turkey that seem to crop up on restaurant menus with greater frequency these days. A variety of factors can increase the chances of your feral entrée tasting "off." How old was the pheasant now glistening under glass? Was your elk left tough and stringy by a physically taxing life? Was the wild boar in rut when it was shot? By far the most important factor, however, is the late animal's diet. Generally speaking, our palates prefer to eat things that eat things our palates prefer to eat. A domesticated goose, for example, that has enjoyed a steady, uniform diet of corn or rice will almost invariably taste less gamy than a wild Canada goose that has had to forage widely among piquant grubs and insects and bitter nuts. The same thing goes for an apple-and-oat-fed deer over one that has nibbled on bitter sage. So can *gamy* be pegged to a specific chemical? It's not a terribly well-studied question, but scientists have isolated a number of specific compounds that contribute to the "strong flavor profile" of venison, goat, and mutton, among other gamy-tasting meats. Foremost among these compounds are two enormously potent *branched fatty acids,* 4-methyloctanoic and 4-methylnonanoic. "We can smell and taste 4-methyloctanoic acid at .006 parts per million," notes flavor chemist Charlotte Brennand of Utah State University. "A little goes a long, long way."

Q What's the oldest-living creature on earth?

—Annie Purcell, Edinburgh, Scotland

A The jury's still out on this one, as crack teams of gerontologists comb the planet in search of superlatives, but there are a few leading candidates. The Galápagos turtle, a perennial favorite, logs an estimated average life span of 90 years—impressive, but still a runner-up to the South Pacific's famously unfishy-tasting fish known as the orange roughy, which has been shown to live as long as 150 years. (How do we know this? It has a tiny bone in its ear that accumulates annual growth rings.) Soon the prize for senescence could shift to a certain sea anemone found in the Bahamas that might be an incredible 2,100 years old, according to initial carbon-14 readings taken from the anemone's secreted horny exoskeleton. Increasing attention has been trained on several species of tube worms recently found in far-flung locations along thermal vents on the ocean floor. Marine biologists believe these tube worms are in excess of 200 years old, but unlike the orange roughy, they don't come with convenient onboard dating devices. Among mammals, humans take the prize: Assuming Methuselah was a case of biblical exaggeration, the oldest documented human was Jeanne Calment, a French woman who died in 1997 at the age of 122.

It shouldn't be too surprising that plants, with their decidedly less complex physiology, win the age game hands down, thanks to several astonishingly decrepit individuals. Witness the *Rhizocarpon geographicum,* a 12,000-year-old lichen growing in Alaska's Brooks Range; a creosote plant in California that's been dated to 11,700 years old; and— drumroll, please—the king's holly, a 40,000-year-old shrub recently discovered in a desolate gully in southwestern Tasmania. If you hear of anything older, please contact Willard Scott.

humans in nature, nature in humans

homo imperfectus

Deficits and design flaws of human physiology

Q My boyfriend always sneezes when he emerges from a theater on a sunny day. Why is this?

—*Nanci Kulig, Philadelphia, Pennsylvania*

A Most likely he has a little something called *photic sneeze reflex* (PSR), an untreatable hereditary condition that affects up to 20 percent of Americans. Its cause is unknown, although some researchers think it involves a neurological short circuit linking the retina and the nose. For people with PSR, any sudden exposure to bright light can trigger a fit of as many as fifteen sneezes.

The occasional nasal eruption is, for most of us, a mere inconvenience. But for certain people, like fighter pilots, it can be lethal. "If you're landing a plane or you're in a dog-fight and you turn into the sun and have to sneeze, that could be dangerous," says Lieutenant Colonel Ray Breiten-bach, an air force reserve doctor and PSR sufferer who has studied the phenomenon. Breitenbach tested whether high-tech tinted goggles help stop the sneezing. (They don't.) He plans to conduct a study in which he'll treat air force cadets to a movie and then wait outside the theater as they emerge. Instead of calling out "Gesundheit," he'll be scrib-bling notes, trying to spot aviation disasters in the making.

Q Why does the skin on our fingers turn pruney in water? Does it hurt anything?

—Jasper Adams, Savannah, Georgia

A Unlike the rest of the epidermis, our fingers are wrapped in a thin, dry outer layer of skin called the *stratum corneum.* Oddly enough, this tissue exhibits many of the same qualities found in animal horn. (Dermatolo-gists refer to it as the *horny layer,* but we won't go into that.) The pertinent point here is that the stratum corneum is dead skin, and it's porous. During a prolonged pool workout or hot-tub session, water molecules insinuate themselves into the dry tissue of the stratum corneum, causing it to stretch and expand. The result is a raisiny effect that more or less follows the peculiar whorl patterns of our fingerprints. But don't worry, Madge: it's tempo-rary, it's harmless, and it's only skin-deep.

Q Why do some people experience weird muscle spasms before falling asleep?

—R. Bruneau and J. Wright, Atlanta, Georgia

A These curious but thoroughly common episodes are known as *hypnic jerks,* but sleep experts don't entirely agree on what causes them. It is known that as we drift headlong toward deep slumber, our various muscle groups gradually relax until they actually become paralyzed, a self-preservation feature common among most mammals that prevents us from acting out our craziest dreams and thus injuring ourselves by pointlessly thrashing about. But early on, as we move from Stage 1 toward REM (rapid eye movement) sleep, there's a window in the transitional process during which our motor functioning is still vaguely up and running, and the line between our brains and our muscles, though fizzling fast, still carries a live signal. Hypnic jerks happen during this twilight zone of repose. Neurologists say that these little spasms are most often caused by anxiety, stress, or a bothersome thought that suddenly yanks us back from the brink of sleep, with our muscles responding in kind by reflexively surging into their wakeful state. Other neurologists suggest that hypnic jerks might at times be the result of our semifunctional muscles attempting to perform the evening's inaugural dream; whatever we're doing in our visions, we're trying to do with our arms and legs, but our neurological circuitry can't quite bring it off. These spasmodic outbursts, though completely normal, can be violent enough to jar us awake or, in extremely rare cases, cause us to break bones. (At the other end of the same neurological spectrum, however, is a class of maladies called *REM behavior disorders,* in which the afflicted sometimes carry out extremely violent acts, even murder, while in the deepest fathoms of slumber.) By the way, a day of extreme physical exertion seems to be an especially good recipe for an outbreak of hypnic jerks. As we settle into sleep after a full day of, say, canoeing, the mind replays the rhythms of the paddling, and our muscles seem to reply in a feeble pantomime. "It's a kind of after-image," suggests Denver sleep specialist Dr. Robert Ballard. "With any repetitive athletic activity, you're firing the same area of your motor cortex, over and over again. It takes awhile for all that electrical activity to simmer down for the night."

Q What causes knuckles to crack? Does it damage anything?
—*Allen McBride, Munford, Alabama*

A Knuckle cracking remains one of our great anatomical puzzles. Although it's not entirely understood, here's what experts do know: The joints of our body are lubricated with an oozy liquid known as *synovial fluid,* sort of the WD-40 of the skeletal system. It's believed that sharply bending and twisting our fingers can cause the synovial fluid to squirt from one side of the knuckle to the other. "Studies suggest that the distinctive popping noise is caused when various gases rush in to fill the empty space left behind by the displaced fluid," explains Dr. Steven Green, of New York's Hospital for Joint Diseases. Mildly repulsive, yes, but surprisingly innocuous, as the fluid soon drains back into position. Green refutes the age-old warning that arthritis and swollen joints will beset the dedicated knuckle cruncher in later life. "As far as we know knuckle cracking leads to nothing harmful," he declares, "except maybe nasty looks from the person beside you."

Q When there is no apparent cause, such as poison oak or an insect bite, why does skin itch? And why does it feel good to scratch?

—Erika Huddleston, Idyllwild, California

A Lots of things make us itch, from histamine-releasing chemical reactions to the patter of tiny insect feet. When there's no apparent culprit, the cause is usually dry skin. "Parched and cracked skin loses flexibility," explains dermatologist Larry Millikan of the Tulane Medical Center. "When you move, it tugs on the skin and twitches all the little nerve endings." That twitch is the itch. Scratching, of course, doesn't really improve the situation, but it does send a lot of competing messages via the same nerves, enough to drown out the itching message at least for a short while. The problem is that scratching can do further damage, and the healing process itself can cause more itching. Like your mom always said, if you keep picking at it, it'll never get better.

Q What good are goose bumps?
—Angie Roland, Salt Lake City, Utah

A None whatsoever. You'd have to be a stunningly hairy guy—Howard Stern or somebody—to get anything useful out of them. Goose bumps are a vestige of the days when we all had pelts. Attached to every hair follicle is a tiny muscle called the *pilo erector*. When you get the willies or the shivers, this muscle pulls on the hair, so it stands on end. This is good if you're an animal: It makes you look bigger and more ferocious. It also keeps you warmer by trapping dead air. In humans, however, all it does is make us look like something from the poultry case.

Q Eating red meat makes me dream weird. Do others share this affliction?
—Ron Ginger, Boulder, Colorado

A Affliction? Weird dreams are God's way of apologizing for having created logic. It's a widely held belief that eating, say, a juicy T-bone or prime rib for dinner will make your evening's in-flight entertainment odder than usual. There might be some truth to it, but it has nothing to do with any specific chemicals in the meat itself. "A lot of people believe that what they eat directly determines or at least influences their dream content," notes Harvard dream expert J. Allan Hobson, "but there's absolutely no evidence for it."

However, red meat is, for many people, notoriously hard to digest. Most likely all that's happening is that you're having trouble breaking down that big steak. Throughout the night, the gastric activity is repeatedly waking you up while visions are still dancing in your head. The more details you can recall, the stranger your dreams are going to seem—because, as Hobson puts it, "Dreams are *normally* weird." It's just that indigestion is giving you a clearer glimpse of the Fellini films that regularly play up there. So next time, skip the Tagamet and enjoy the show.

Q Is it true that a great fright can cause your hair to turn gray suddenly?

—Margo Stratton, Minneapolis, Minnesota

A There is a large body of blanched-hair folktales out there—dubious-sounding anecdotes associated with the traumas of war, natural catastrophes, maulings by grizzlies, and other moments of intense horror. (Barbara Bush, for example, is rumored to have silvered from the shock of a daughter's sudden death.) Such stories notwithstanding, it's a woefully understudied phenomenon, and many hair biologists suspect it doesn't happen at all, at least not with the dramatic immediacy depicted in horror flicks. Prevailing medical opinion suggests that people who claim their hair turned white "overnight" are mistaken about the time line. Experts agree that most documented cases of rapid hair whitening can be attributed to a rare form of *alopecia areata*, a genetic autoimmune disease in which T cells mistake hair follicles for a foreign substance and launch an aggressive counterattack that results in partial or complete baldness. On such occasions, the immune system inexplicably targets only pigmented hairs, causing them to fall out, whereas gray hairs, which are often colorless and thus might be far more numerous than a person realizes, stay put. It's a shedding process that happens not in a single night but over a period of weeks or months, leaving behind a patchier version of the Phil Donahue corona. How this odd self-allergy is linked to stress is still a mystery. "Emotional trauma may throw your immune system off-kilter," posits Rose Kozar of the National Alopecia Areata Foundation, "which can trigger a predisposition for a disease that you never knew you had."

Q I've heard the warnings, but now I want the truth: is it dangerous to hold in a sneeze?

—J. Weidner, Toronto, Canada

A People who've attempted sneezus interruptus have invariably regretted it. It's a stupid thing to do and can even, in rare instances, kill you. When you sneeze, you're expelling aerosol particles at a speed of more than one hundred feet per second, a force akin to that of a fire hose. You need all of this force for a reason, of course. It's nature's way of clearing out any debris—pollen, dirt, dander, or, if you're a kid, lunchroom milk—that might be lodged in your sinuses and nasal tract. By and large, it's an effective mechanism, so effective that thousands of creatures throughout the animal kingdom, from parrots to ferrets to iguanas, have developed it. Holding in a sneeze, which is not a very easy thing to bring off in the first place, violates millions of years of evolutionary biology, directing all that aforementioned force *inward,* thus creating a nasal cavity implosion. *Sneeze abortions,* as the experts call them, have been known to cause fractures in the nasal cartilage, major nosebleeds, burst eardrums, broken blood vessels in the eye, detached retinas, even fatal strokes. If you happen to be sick, holding in a sneeze can drive millions of tiny pathogenic particles deep into the sinus tissues, which can lead to serious infections. Alternatively, it can force air under the skin, causing a condition known as *facial emphysema.* Gruesome outcomes all, and compelling proof that the only safe sneeze is an explosive one.

not ready

almost there

ready to mate.

Q What are the evolutionary reasons for, and possible benefits of, male-pattern baldness?

—Tom Ruttan, Woodstock, Ontario, Canada

A Male-pattern baldness involves a combination of genetics and testosterone. To oversimplify slightly, if you're cursed with a certain gene, which perversely enough is passed down through your mother, then your balls will make your hair fall out. The same set of chemical signals, conversely, puts hair on your chest and props up the multibillion-dollar razor-blade industry. Why does nature bother with all of these elaborate hair reallocations? The best guess is that balding evolved as a way for males to show females that they were mature and hormonally sound. "There tend to be a lot of things that signal age," says biological anthropologist Jim Moore of the University of California, San Diego. "They show that you've got good genes, because you've survived. And the testosterone connection shows you're ready to reproduce." All the same, you might have noticed that the signal seems have gotten mixed up somewhere along the way; apparently tone-deaf to thousands of years of evolution, most women fail to respond to male baldness in the way they're "supposed" to. That's not biology, that's just life.

For a long time it was thought that male-pattern baldness was unique to humans, but it's not: the stump-tailed

humans in nature, nature in humans

macaque, a monkey native to India, South China, and the Malay Peninsula, seems to go bald for similar genetic reasons, though no one has yet spotted middle-aged male macaques swirling that proverbial last strand around and around.

Q Why is yawning contagious?
—*Barbara Billings, Eugene, Oregon*

A First, let us dispense with the antiquated notion that a yawn is the body's attempt to pump extra oxygen into our fatigued systems. Scientists have shown that a person in an oxygen chamber yawns just as much as anyone else. No, yawning seems to be tied to more primal purposes, with contagion at the center of it. A semiautomatic reflex that originates in the brain stem and marks transitions from one mental state to another, yawning is widespread throughout the animal kingdom, particularly among carnivores. Watch a pride of lions: when one cat opens its mouth, pretty soon there's an outbreak. Although the precise mechanism for its contagiousness remains unknown, yawning appears to be a piece of ancient genetic wiring meant to help synchronize clan behavior, a form of prelinguistic communication indicating that it's time to move on to the next big thing. Think of it as a way for, say, a Neanderthal to let his comrades know that the nap's over; let's go bag us a woolly mammoth.

Q What purpose do male nipples serve?

—Rolf Spencer, Norfolk, Virginia

A If you're asking "What is the evolutionary advantage?" the answer is probably none. You got your nipples in your first few months as a fetus, back when you were anatomically indistinguishable from a little girl. At about fourteen weeks, hormones kicked in and caused you to develop your standard, factory-issue male parts. The nipples stayed, though. It would be too much trouble to suppress them, and besides, they don't do any harm.

Actually, there's no compelling reason why males *can't* give milk. Men are equipped with small mammary glands and ducts; all that's missing are the hormones to make them work. But there are certain rare hormonal imbalances that are known to enlarge male mammary glands, and there have even been a few reported cases of illnesses that caused men to lactate.

What about other mammals? In July 1992 a team of biologists working in Malaysia discovered that male Dayak fruit bats were producing milk, possibly to nurse their young. (Noticing that the male nipples were unusually large, the biologists gave them a little squeeze—and voilà.) This is the first case of male lactation ever documented in the wild. As the phenomenon is subjected to further study, we can only hope for answers to the burning question: are Dayak fruit bats suffering from some kind of endocrine dysfunction—or are they just extremely family-oriented males?

humans in nature, nature in humans

Q Why do I often feel like I'm going to get sick right after strenuous exercise?

—Jon Godin, Acton, Massachusetts

A To risk stating the obvious, the desire to barf after a one-hundred-yard dash is the body's way of telling us that we've overdone it—yet sports physiologists can't seem to agree on how it happens. It might be related to blood-glucose depletion or a temporary imbalance in the nervous system. Another theory: During intense anaerobic activity, muscles in the gut can clamp down and constrict the flow of blood, throwing one's metabolism out of whack. "It's like standing on a hose," explains Craig Horswill of the Gatorade Sports Science Institute. "Take your foot off, and you have an initial blast of water before the pressure returns to normal." Scientists also believe there's a psychological dimension to postexertion nausea—a result of the nervous energy that builds up before a big race. "Athletes vomit most when the stakes are high," notes Horswill. "It's the equivalent of stage fright." Only messier.

Q I hit my funny bone frequently, so I have to ask: What is it, and where's the humor?

—Janice Garcia, Troy, New York

A It's a double misnomer, actually. The funny bone is not a bone, and as some repeat sufferers who've ultimately required surgery will tell you, it's not at all funny. The important thing to understand is that the funny bone—also known as the crazy bone in some precincts—is a neurological problem, not an orthopedic one. That tingly, hot-acid sensation we sometimes feel when we bang the inside of our elbows is actually a nerve—the *ulnar nerve*—being struck or compressed. The ulnar is a very long sensory and motor nerve that runs from the shoulder down to our ring and pinky fingers. It's responsible for, among other things, grip and dexterity in the *intrinsic* muscles of the hand. The problem is, the ulnar runs painfully close to the skin at the elbow. Knock it just so and you'll squash the exposed nerve against hard bone, momentarily interrupting the nerve impulse and generating a kind of electric shock that shoots all the way to the fingertips—the physiological equivalent of striking a power main. Think of the funny bone as an anatomical design flaw suffered by some of us in the upper registers of the animal kingdom (other primates such as chimpanzees and orangutans apparently experience the same problem). It's nature's way of punishing us for the hubris of sprouting arms.

outlore

Dubious figures and indubitable facts of natural history

Q Where did the name "America" come from? I seem to recall an explorer named Amerigo Verspucci, but if the entire Western Hemisphere was named after him, why isn't he more famous?

—Katie Burford, Irvine, California

A You remember right. For better or worse— probably worse—the New World was named after Florentine nobleman Amerigo Vespucci (1454–1512). A contemporary of Christopher Columbus who helped finance and outfit numerous exploratory voyages,

Vespucci was a so-so mariner who racked up a hat trick of expeditions to the Nuovo Mondo, but always as a passenger or as a minor officer—never as a ship's commander. To his credit, however, he was a fine writer and a meticulous field cartographer, and dispatches of his 1499 voyage to what is now Guyana circulated widely in Europe. Among his avid readers was Martin Waldseemüller, a German cartographer who in 1507 decided to honor Vespucci by labeling the New World *America,* the feminized and Latinized form of *Amerigo.* (*Amerigo* is Italian for *Henry,* so technically speaking, we live in the United States of Henrietta.) In a later edition of his map, Waldseemüller thought better of it and reverted to the noncommittal Terra Incognita, but by then the damage was done and the moniker—however dubiously conceived—had begun to stick. God Bless Henrietta!

Q Was Indiana Jones based on a real person?

—Gail Alberta, Mill Valley, California

A Any archaeology department worth its salt has at least one professor eager to take credit for inspiring the Lucas/Spielberg hero. The most commonly touted model is the late Roy Chapman Andrews, who led the American Museum of Natural History's 1920s expedition to the Gobi Desert. He discovered the first fossil dinosaur eggs, but he never fled a cave pursued by a malevolent boulder. Vendyl Jones, an archaeologist in Israel, and Roy

Mackal, a Chicago cryptozoologist, are also oft cited, as is Montana paleontologist Jack Horner. For his part, Lucas insists Indy is an original. "We have no confirmation of real-life models," says a slightly testy spokeswoman at Lucasfilm Ltd. "Look, it's only a movie."

Q Who murdered explorer Meriwether Lewis, and why?
—Chris Cali, Silver Lake, Michigan

A On October 10, 1809, three years after returning from his historic expedition, the thirty-five-year-old governor of the Louisiana Territory stopped at a home on the Natchez Trace in Tennessee. That night he was shot. Various accounts have suggested that he was murdered, either in the course of a robbery or as part of a conspiracy that allegedly reached all the way to Washington.

Yet most historians believe that Lewis committed suicide, shooting himself in the head and chest with a pair of pistols. One account claims he survived long enough to declare: "I have done the business, my good servant. Give me some water."

Unlike William Clark, who became a powerful landowner and lived a long, prosperous life, Lewis couldn't get into the swing of things after the great expedition. Unsuccessful in love and real estate, wracked with malaria and possibly syphilis, and all too friendly with the bottle, Lewis was unable to finish his memoirs. Think of him as Bernstein to Clark's Woodward.

James Starrs, a forensic scientist who once used ground-penetrating radar to study the skulls of Lizzie Borden's parents, has proposed a plan to exhume Lewis's bones from his Tennessee grave and settle the matter. Starrs has his own theory. "A two-shot suicide by a man handy with weapons is not a typical suicide," he says, "so my working hypothesis is homicide."

Q Why are bats associated with the occult?

—Molly Stephens, Santa Barbara, California

A The Western world's wholesale demonization of this order of mammals dates back to the Old Testament's Book of Leviticus, in which God warned against eating bats and other "unclean fowls." Shakespeare ratcheted the noir atmospherics a notch with his famous "toe of frog, wool of bat" witch-talk in *Macbeth*. And things only got worse when Bram Stoker's blood-slurping Count Dracula arrived on the scene in 1897. (In truth, vampire bats account for less than half of 1 percent of all chiropterans and prefer bovine blood over ours any day.) Of course, bats' veiny wings, ratlike body, and nocturnal habits never did much for their reputation. "Until the invention of the lightbulb, we seldom went out at night, so bats were shrouded in mystery," explains University of Tennessee bat expert Gary F. McCracken. "But now that we've learned what they do through night vision and radio telemetry, it's helped their public image tremendously." Of late, the bat has been gaining favor for its ability to devour five thousand mosquitoes in a single night—reason, perhaps, why in parts of Asia, it's a symbol for happiness and good fortune.

Q How did Henry David Thoreau pronounce his name: Tho-roo or Tho-roe?

—Y. Littlefield, New York, New York

A Neither. Try THOR-o, accent on the first syllable. Nineteenth-century Americans yearned to sound European, and Tho-roe was their best guess at how a Frenchman would have pronounced the name. However, an aunt of Thoreau's called this mispronunciation "ludicrous."

By the way, our man on Walden Pond wasn't actually named Henry David; he was David Henry. For some reason he changed the order after college. Apparently, many of his Massachusetts acquaintances felt this was a snooty affectation. "His name ain't Henry D. Thoreau, and everybody knows it," one neighboring Concord farmer is reported to have ranted after the change. And people wonder why the poor guy wanted to be alone in the woods.

Q In the movie *The Edge*, Anthony
Hopkins makes a "compass" by
rubbing a paper clip on a silk shirt
and then floating it, atop a leaf,
in water. Does this work?

—C. Rogers, Akron, Ohio

A Ah, the old silk shirt trick. Although this is theoretically possible, screenwriter David Mamet took some
liberties in crafting that scene. Twelfth-century Chinese
mariners, who are credited with devising the first compass, would place a sliver of lodestone on a floating stick
and watch it swivel into alignment with the poles. The
magnetic field of a lodestone, however, is far stronger than
the electric charge of a flimsy piece of staticky metal. Not
only that, but a leaf would make a wobbly platform for
our makeshift needle, and ripples in the water would render it practically useless—which might explain why Hopkins spent much of the movie lost in the bush.

Q Why do we christen boats with
bottles of champagne?

—Emma Murdoch, Tucson, Arizona

A According to maritime historians, the custom dates
back more than a thousand years to the Vikings, who
are thought to have practiced a gruesome ship-launching
ritual called *roller reddening*. To propitiate the sea gods,
boatwrights would strap a sacrificial maiden onto rollers

used to maneuver ships into the water; the splattering blood ensured a safe voyage. Then someone decided that the gods might enjoy red wine just as much, and maidens everywhere breathed a sigh of relief. It wasn't until the late seventeenth century, when a Benedictine monk named Dom Pierre Pérignon produced the first bottle of sparkling wine, that champagne came into vogue as a christening libation. The tradition got a big boost in 1912 with the sinking of the *Titanic,* whose owners apparently tempted fate by neglecting to smash her with the ceremonial magnum—or, for that matter, blood or wine. Bottoms up!

high camp

Sage counsel for backroad and backcountry

Q Whenever I hike for a long time, my hands get numb. What's wrong?

—James White, Omaha, Nebraska

A Fear not—this is a common vexation that's both simply caused and simply alleviated. When you walk with your arms dangling at your sides for long periods, the steady pendulum-like motion creates just enough centrifugal force to drive the blood downward toward your hands—and keep it there. Because your muscles aren't contracting enough to offset this pressure, the blood in your fingers has to fight gravity to make its way back to your heart. (Notice that runners seldom report this problem because their stride requires more movement of the arms and greater flexion of the elbows.) As the blood pools in your hands, it causes your fingers to become swollen and ruddy. Eventually you get that weird tingling sensation, caused by a lack of oxygen in the blood and also by the swelling itself (which slightly compresses the nerve endings of your fingers). The problem can be greatly exacerbated if you're wearing a backpack with shoulder straps that are too tightly adjusted. The remedy for hiker's hands? Force yourself to flex your hand muscles as you walk, and occasionally bend your elbows or even raise your arms over your head. "Better yet," suggests Northland College Wilderness specialist Grant White, "just carry a walking stick."

Q Can giardia survive in stream ice?
—*Alan Livingston, Denver, Colorado*

A Yes, at least some can—and when you're talking giardia, known to science as *Giardia lamblia,* some is more than enough. Even a few in your gut will cause a host of famously nasty symptoms. And these protozoa, sad to say, are extremely hardy. When outside a host—as when suspended in a mountain stream—they take the form of tough-shelled microscopic cysts. Cold weather alone doesn't kill them. Freezing can, but only if the cyst gets physically crushed by ice crystals. Don't bet on it. If you want to drink stream ice, filter or heat it first. The water has to reach the giardia's *thermal death point* of 135 degrees Fahrenheit. "Heat it until it begins to steam," says microbiologist Ernest A. Meyer of Oregon Health Sciences University, editor of the forthrightly titled book *Giardiasis*. Then, to be safe, let the water boil. This will not only kill any bacteria present, but will ensure, gratifyingly, that every giardia you've scooped up crosses the great thermal death divide.

Q What is quicksand? Where does it occur? And is it as dangerous as in the movies?

—Christian Timmerman, Phoenix, Arizona

A Quicksand can be found anywhere on Earth, wherever the conditions are right. It's a kind of thick soup created when water flows up through sand. It can develop, for example, along the inland side of a levee when a river is in flood stage or when an underground spring flows beneath a silty bank. The flow can cancel out the weight of the sand. Instead of packing together like a solid, the sand granules float around. When you step into it, there's nothing to support your weight, and you start to sink. However, you won't be pulled under, as victims invariably are in those old jungle flicks. Quicksand is thicker than water, so in the long run you'll float. You probably could drown if you really put your mind to it, but your corpse wouldn't go anywhere.

If you should step in quicksand: Get on your back and let your feet float to the surface. Then squidge slowly to stable land. It'll take time. There are reports of people taking all day to move a half dozen feet in quicksand. You could starve, but you won't sink.

On the other hand, animals that can't float on their back—elephants, for instance—are in real danger of drowning in quicksand. In fact, some researchers believe that the legendary "elephant graveyards" might actually be patches of former bog or quicksand where groups of pachyderms got trapped. In any event, you can ignore the old Tarzan movies: Quicksand can't suck you in. Hollywood's another matter.

Q What would happen if I wore my Gore-Tex jacket inside out in a rainstorm?

—Bill Newman, Prince George, British Columbia, Canada

A You mean besides looking ridiculous? Gore-Tex doesn't care which way you wear it. It's like a sieve that traps water while letting vapor through. As long as you don't plug its pores, it'll do its job. But think of the rest of your jacket. Usually, the Gore-Tex membrane is sandwiched between an outer fabric that sheds water and an inner layer that wicks moisture away from your skin. Reversing things will, as Patagonia spokesman Mike Harrelson puts it, "defeat the garment." The absorbent liner, turned to the elements, will soak up rain, and the jacket will grow heavy. Meanwhile, perspiration will bead up on the water-repellent fabric and soak your shirt. Though your jacket hasn't leaked at all, you'll feel wet, cold, and miserable—which is no way to feel inside clothing that's set you back a few hundred dollars.

Q Why do old tents smell like barf?

—Chip Brown, New York, New York

A People will tell you it's mildew, but they're wrong. Tents do suffer from mildew, of course, but that's another problem and another smell. The real culprit here is cellulose acetate butyrate (CAB), which is commonly added to the polyurethane coatings used on tents. When CAB breaks down over time, one of its many by-products is butyric acid, which gives off a distinctly puky odor. (*Butyric* comes from the Latin word for butter; butyric acid is the substance that gives rancid butter its endearing fragrance.) According to Kris Krishnan, technical director of Raffi & Swanson, a manufacturer of polyurethane coatings, the odor is "not normal—it's an abused condition." You can avoid CAB breakdown by taking a few simple precautions: Keep your tent out of excessive sunlight. Don't store it wet. And don't leave it cooking in your car trunk for weeks at a time.

Q How do you remove leeches? Are they dangerous?

—Todd Kushner, Kuala Lumpur, Malaysia

A Bogart might have demonized them in *The African Queen,* but these hermaphroditic annelids are harmless. Unlike ticks and mosquitoes, leeches don't transmit deadly diseases, and their bite is usually painless, though some species leave a scar that looks remarkably similar to the Mercedes-Benz emblem. True, leeches do have frightening appetites: equipped with some three hundred microscopic teeth that grind away at your flesh, the average leech can slurp up to two tablespoons of blood—about ten times its body mass—in under half an hour.

Since medieval times the leech has been called upon to treat everything from insanity to gout, with varying degrees of success. For clearing up black eyes (a secret that actors have long known about), leeches can't be beat. This talent derives from the leech's impressive stores of salivary anticoagulants, which allow it to suck a meal without clotting interruption. More recently, doctors have used leeches to clean injuries and restore circulation to reattached fingers, toes, and even ears.

So how do you remove one? Try applying salt, moist tobacco, or a lemon wedge until the leech falls off. Otherwise, a brisk flick of the finger might do the trick. Don't try to peel them off, or you'll wind up with a laceration. "But fear not," insists one leech expert we called. "Leeches are your friends."

Q
The "unimproved" roads around here get this weird pattern of regularly spaced ridges running across them. What causes this—wind, water, or extraterrestrials?

—*Monty Olson, Tucson, Arizona*

A That ribbed pattern you're talking about is called *washboarding,* and it's caused neither by wind nor by rain, but, ironically enough, by the very thing that's supposed to make for smoother driving: your car's suspension. All that "quiet ride" technology under your car might feel good to you, but it can be hell on unimproved road surfaces.

Imagine you're driving down a gravel road. You hit a bump, and your car dissipates the shock by bouncing in a rhythmic pattern that engineers call a *harmonic oscillation.* Your car, says Forest Service engineer Tom Pettigrew, a man with a lot of country roads on his hands, becomes "kind of like a trampoline." As your bouncing car digs into the road surface, it displaces gravel and begets even more bumps. Over time, suspensions not varying greatly from car to car, the bumps turn into a series of evenly spaced ridges that can make your steering column rattle like a jackhammer.

Barring some radical change in how suspensions are made, Pettigrew says, washboarding is almost inevitable on unpaved roads that see heavy use. The Forest Service has been working with logging companies to diminish washboarding by experimenting with a new system called *central tire inflation,* in which an onboard computer automatically lets air out of the tires of a big logging truck so that they're nice and squishy. But there's really only one thing the average car driver can do: slow down.

Q How does bug repellent work?
—*Grant Taylor, San Antonio, Texas*

A Experts will tell you that only one thing repels mosquitoes, blackflies, and other bloodsucking bugs with any lasting efficacy—a yellowish, synthetic chemical called N, N- diethyl-m-toluamide, more commonly known as DEET. Developed by Agriculture Department chemists in the late 1940s to protect army troops in malarial jungles, DEET is the active ingredient in most insect repellents sold today—especially the stronger "sportsman" formulas that last for up to four hours and are marketed for serious forays into buggy outbacks. (DEET's potency is infamous: after several widely reported cases of severe skin rashes in the 1980s, EPA tests concluded that the chemical, in large quantities, can cause allergic reactions but is noncarcinogenic.) What's especially cool about DEET is that, strictly speaking, it's not a repellent at all; it's a sly and sophisticated substance, a chemical saboteur that effectively jams a mosquito's onboard radar system and temporarily shuts it down. To understand how it works, you have to understand how mosquitoes are attracted to you in the first place. Depending on how the wind is blowing, they can sense your presence from as far away as seventy feet, their antennae receptors detecting the invisible miasma of exhaled carbon dioxide that permanently hovers over you, much like Pigpen's stinkcloud in *Peanuts*. The closer a mosquito gets to you, the more rapidly these receptors fire, until finally the little vermin lands on your skin and prepares to do what it does best: *bloodfeed*. DEET doesn't mask your presence, not exactly. If you're slathered with the stuff, mosquitoes will still be drawn to you, keying in on your carbon dioxide exhalations as always and sometimes even lighting on your skin, hunting for a warm spot where the blood thrums close to the surface. But then something curious happens. The DEET (rising off your body in steady fumes) begins to bond to the mosquito's antennae receptors and assails them. Befuddled by this new stimulus, the bug doesn't know what to do next. It just thumps around, trying in vain to get a clear signal somewhere in all this sensory din. "DEET neither hurts nor repels mosquitoes, it simply overwhelms them," says Jonathan Day, a University of Florida entomologist who's done repellent testing for fifteen years. "The bug can't move on to the next step—that is, biting you—because it's not getting the right chemical cue. It may take a few hours for it to clear its head." A mosquito drunk on DEET is just like the rest of us, suggests Day—"suffering from information overload."

time to chill

Cold realities from the dead of winter

Q Remember in "To Build a Fire," where the guy tries to kill his dog and crawl inside to warm up? Would that work?

—*Gus FitzGerald, Cleveland, Ohio*

A Jack London's anonymous protagonist wasn't trying to shove his entire body into his dog's innards—just his hands, to warm them up so he could strike his matches. And though this trick probably would have worked, he would have gotten a lot more warmth from his dog if he'd just snuggled with him.

Other lore has suggested crawling into a bigger creature—an elk or buffalo or whatever's handy—but it's just not practical. Getting inside an animal is a lot of work. Soaked with the beast's body fluids, you'd become hypothermic in minutes. And in the sixty-below weather that London was describing, even a big animal would freeze fast, so the benefits would be short-lived.

Experts at the Army's Northern Warfare Training Center in Alaska say London's character should have put his hands, matches, and tinder into his armpits or his crotch to warm them up. London should have known this basic arctic survival tip, as he'd traveled to the Yukon, but he was sailing in the Tropics when he wrote "To Build a Fire." That's the trouble with sunshine and surf: it makes you forget.

Q It's said that no two snowflakes are alike. How do they know this?

—Brianna Simms, Spokane, Washington

A A good number of scientists, such as William P. Wergin at Maryland's Natural Resources Institute, have examined countless snowflakes under electron microscopes. So far, no one has found the magic twins. There are sound scientific reasons why this is so. Every snowflake starts out looking pretty much the same: a simple hexagonal crystal that forms on a particle of dust. But as it falls through a cloud, it grows and changes form dramatically. Depending on how cold and moist it is inside the cloud, a snowflake can assume the shape of a plate, a star, or a hexagonal pillar. As it descends, it tends to grow one way, then another, then another, building on itself in an endlessly complex pattern that combines the various prototypes. Says John Hallett of the Desert Research Institute in Reno, "Two snowflakes would look alike if they followed the exact same trajectory as they fell through the sky—but they don't."

Q Why does hypothermia make people confused, even delirious?
—Wayne Burton, Seoul, South Korea

A Of all the organs of the body, the brain is by far the most sensitive to changes in temperature. A drop of only three degrees Fahrenheit inside the brain's tissues can manifest itself in some notably wacked behavior. "The millions of chemical reactions that routinely go on in your brain slow down in the cold," explains Murray Hamlet, director of operations at the Army Research Institute of Environmental Medicine. "This causes the cells of your central nervous system to stop talking to each other." The downward spiral can be quite abrupt. In the early throes of hypothermia, your motor skills gradually deteriorate (you drop a mitten in the snow and can't readily pick it up). Later you start to make bizarre judgment calls (even if you could retrieve the mitten, you decide you'd rather not). Then you hallucinate. "A hypothermic person might look at the mitten," says Hamlet, "and think it's a bar of soap." By this point, our sluggish brains are receiving bad information. The signals are tainted. Oddly, though—and this is part of hypothermia's insidious advance—we don't recognize how confused we are. Survivors of advanced hypothermia often report that their experience unfolds vividly and rationally, with the insistent internal logic of a clear dream. They are often stunned when they later learn that their interpretation of events was completely off base.

One of the final delirious acts common to victims of terminal hypothermia is the bizarre phenomenon known as *paradoxical undressing*. Very near the end, victims feel suddenly flush and hot and are compelled to remove their clothes. Says Dr. Hamlet: "It's the last thing they ever do."

Q Where does the white go when the snow melts?

—Joe Schmitz, St. Paul, Minnesota

A Not to get all Zen on you, but there isn't any white, so it doesn't go anywhere. Technically speaking, snow isn't white, it's clear. When you get to examining it, granule by granule, you quickly see that frozen water, like its fluid counterpart, is colorless. To understand why snow looks white, consider an ice cube: You look at it from some angles, and it's transparent. From other angles it shines, which means it's reflecting light. Now, snow consists of zillions of minuscule ice crystals, and each one of them acts like the cube, sometimes bouncing the light, sometimes letting it through. But there are so many crystals, and they're so small and randomly heaped together, that ultimately almost all the light that hits the snow is scattered and reflected back. That's pretty much the definition of whiteness. When it melts into water, snow loses the crystalline structure with its attendant light-scattering properties.

All this, of course, applies to the country kind of snow. For urban slush, the question is where the gray goes, and the answer is simple: it's ubiquitous—on cars, on buildings, on surfaces everywhere—an unlovely film of diesel fumes, rubber residue, cinders, and various kinds of dinge better left unspecified.

Q How does dew form, and why does it seem to collect only in the early morning?

—Euclidia Arnold, Oxford, England

A To understand dew—as well as its cold-weather sibling, frost—you first have to grasp this universal meteorological truth: The chillier the air, the less water vapor it can hold. As the mercury inches downward, every swath of air will eventually reach a point at which it can no longer retain moisture in a vaporous state and thus must unload its watery ballast on the ground. Your Eyewitness News Accu-Doppler Weatherman calls this the *dew point,* and though it varies according to how generally humid the air is, the dew point always occurs during the coolest part in the day—in the early morning hours, usually. The other important thing to understand is that dew is an extremely localized phenomenon, the by-product of a fragile microclimate that sets up just a few millimeters above the ground as the temperature plummets overnight. Because the ground is a solid, and because all solids rapidly radiate temperature changes, the thin pocket of air immediately touching the ground cools off especially quickly after sundown. "By early morning, the air lying along the ground may be as much as twenty degrees cooler than the air that's just three feet up," notes Dr. Richard Armstrong of the National Snow and Ice Data Center. "It's in this narrow band, with its steep temperature gradient, where all the action takes place." The final ingredient you need for dew or frost is prolonged stillness. The slightest overnight breeze can churn things up enough to prevent the formation of this paper-thin, terrain-hugging microclimate. Which is why Florida citrus growers often keep enormous fans blowing in their groves through the winter and early spring to forestall a crop-devastating frost.

Q Why do women feel cold sooner than men?

—Betsy Bartel, Bellvue, Colorado

A This is one of those weird perception-versus-reality deals that's hard to parse. First the reality part: Women do tend to have a greater ratio of surface area to body mass than do men, so they lose heat faster. And women are four times more likely than men to develop Raynaud's disease, a malady in which blood vessels in the extremities suddenly constrict, causing fingers and toes to blanch and grow exaggeratedly cold. But curiously, far fewer women suffer frostbite or freeze to death than men. Why? Here's where the perception part comes in: Dr. Murray Hamlet of the Army Research Institute of Environmental Medicine raises the intriguing possibility that women might just have a more finely tuned survival mechanism. Another way of putting it: When it comes to cold, maybe women are just *smarter.* "If we stuck our hands in ice water at the same time, I'd probably be able to keep mine in longer than the average woman would," he says. "Is it because her blood vessels constrict sooner, or because she perceives cold sooner? Perception, I'd say, is the better part of survival."

Q How thick does ice have to be to hold your weight safely? Is there some kind of mathematical formula you can use to be sure?

—Meg Larimer, Oxford, England

A The public safety people up in Grand Rapids, Minnesota, who are on exceedingly familiar terms with this subject, say that although there's no such thing, technically speaking, as a foolproof formula for guaranteeing the safety of ice, there are some pretty good rules of thumb: First of all, stay away from any ice that looks milky or bubbly or streaked. What you're looking for is a perfectly clear, uniformly solid sheet. Always avoid slush and ice that form over moving water—streams, currents, or spots where springs feed into ponds or lakes. Don't proceed on ice that's burdened with heavy snow, and steer clear of *pressure ridges,* the jagged fracture lines that build up, especially on large lakes or Arctic seas, when two large drifting ice plates bump against one another. (Eskimos have been known to disappear while camping along these fracture lines, which are known in the Arctic as *ivus.*) The pressure becomes so powerful in an ivu that an imperceptible shift in the ice can cause the ridge to crumple suddenly, swallowing up anyone or anything that might be nearby.) The Minnesota Department of Natural Resources advises that you bring along an ice auger and test for thickness according to the following guidelines: Two inches or less, stay off. Four inches means it's safe to lace up the skates. Five inches is strong enough for a snowmobile or all-terrain vehicle. Eight to twelve inches will support a car or small pickup, and twelve to fifteen inches can withstand the weight of a medium-size truck. Not to dwell on the morbid, but if you're going to drive on ice, keep your seatbelts unbuckled and your windows rolled down. Oh, and one last safety tip, generally ignored by ice fishermen of the Great White North: go easy on the Molsons, eh?

Q What makes snow squeak when you walk on it?

—Ann Franklin, St. Louis, Missouri

A It might be comforting to know that there are people in the world who spend large amounts of time peering through microscopes at dainty flakes of snow. What we've learned from these glaciologists is that in particularly chilly temperatures—roughly twenty degrees Fahrenheit or colder—soft, wet snowflakes harden into abrasive ice crystals. That high-pitched, clean-sounding crunch we all know so well is the collective sound of untold thousands of these tiny ice granules rubbing against each other when compressed under the weight of your foot. As the temperature rises, the flakes' molecular structure becomes flexible and a lubricating layer of water develops, leaving us with a stoic substance that—no matter what kind of boot-stomping duress we put it under—will not squeal.

Q Why do tongues stick to cold metal?

—Paul McDonald, Austin, Texas

A You need to be extremely careful where you put your tongue, and this is especially true during the winter months. There are stories of mortified skiers unable to disembark from ski lifts because their tongues were freeze-dried to the metal safety bar. It's not only our tongue that manifests

this humiliating tendency to bond to cold surfaces—it's any warm, wet body part. A simple gloveless hand often has enough moisture in it to adhere to a frozen doorknob; and if your fingers happen to be slightly wet with, say, dishwater, then the Bondo-effect is virtually guaranteed, with the extra wetness serving as an instant Krazy Glue. "Your body part becomes 'flash frozen' to the cold object," notes geochemist John Kelley of the University of Alaska, Fairbanks. "Because metal is such a good conductor, the heat of your body is immediately transferred, and all surface moisture becomes crystallized." The result can be contact frostbite, best left to rewarm on its own, or torn skin cells, best treated by a physician. The classic treatment is to pour warm water (if you happen to have any) on the compromised appendage. This will melt the ice crystals, but will do little to restore your sense of pride.

worldlywise

terra informa

Q What are the Seven Natual Wonders of the World?

—Jennifer Murphy, Northampton, Massachusetts

A This just in: There aren't *any* natural wonders of the world, let alone seven. At least not officially. It's remarkable how completely this popular notion has become enshrined in our thinking, as though some tribunal of white-wigged geographers meets in The Hague every so often to update the world's scenic Leader Board. "Grand Canyon has just overtaken Blue Grotto of Capri for the number 5 position!" Although practically every roadside waterfall or freak rock formation in America touts itself as one of the seven natural wonders of the world, or even more tantalizingly, "the eighth natural wonder," there is no sanctioned roster and never has been. It's all just marketing hokum. "From a tourism point of view, it's advantageous to advertise your claim to be such a site," explains Roger Payne of the U.S. Board on Geographic Names. "But the fact is, there is no official list." True, the phrase has an undeniable resonance, playing as it does off the venerable concept of the Seven Wonders of the Ancient World (the Hanging Gardens of Babylon, the Colossus of Rhodes, the Giza Pyramids, and so on), a classical septet of architectural achievements first suggested by the Greek historian Herodotus around 400 B.C. that went through several subsequent refinements. Although the Greeks failed to follow up with a pantheon of natural wonders, there are several contemporary lists that do nature's star attractions some justice. With the recent addition of the Golden Mountains of Russia, the United Nations roster of World Heritage Sites (locales having "universal value from the point of history, art, or science") has swelled to an unruly 582 and counting. And the National Park Service has tapped some 587 significant places in America, such as the Palisades of the Hudson, as national natural landmarks. Despite these seemingly comprehensive registers, some sites still cling to the notion that they belong among a mystic and essential Big Seven. When we asked Natural Bridge of Virginia marketing director David Parker which authority bestowed the span's fancy superlative ("One of the Seven Natural Wonders of the World!" proclaims its glossy brochure), he conceded, somewhat sheepishly, "I couldn't tell you in my wildest dreams."

Cartographic crannies and continental quirks

Q Why is Europe considered a continent?

—Max Jenks, Madison, Wisconsin

A A continent is defined as "a large, continuous mass of land," though how large and how continuous are open to interpretation. The line of size demarcation falls somewhere between Australia (the world's smallest continent) and Greenland (the largest island). Europe meets the size definition; it's the continuity criterion that creates problems, for a casual glance at a map tells you that Europe is really only a western addendum to Asia. Although some professional cartographers use the term *Eurasia,* most consider the Ural Mountains, which extend from the Arctic Ocean to the Caspian Sea, a boundary of continental proportions. Perhaps, but Europe's lofty landmass status still seems specious somehow (as does the term *continental breakfast*). When we asked a spokesman at atlas-publisher Rand McNally about this, he began to free-associate: "It's a gestalt, if you will. The cartographers looked at huge chunks of land and said, 'That's the way it is.' Some things we can't explain, despite all our education."

Q How was Ayers Rock formed?

—Mory McCabe, Virginia City, Nevada

A Ayers Rock is a hulking monolith of sandstone—a mile and a half long and 1,143 feet high—that rises from the semiarid desert of Australia's Northern Territory. It's an anomaly, unrelated to a broader mountain range or a long-ago volcanic eruption. Aborigines call it Uluru and consider it sacred. They attribute its creation to the handiwork of ancestors. But to geologists, Ayers Rock is a prime example of a rare formation known as a *bornhardt*. Like other well-known bornhardts, such as Georgia's Stone Mountain, Ayers Rock sits atop a trough in the earth's surface, an unusual geological placement that over time compressed the normally porous sandstone, making it extremely hard and almost completely weather resistant. It's rather like a diamond embedded in the sand. Ayers Rock withstood one hundred million years of erosion while everything around it crumbled into dust and blew away—reason enough to deserve our respect.

Q Is the sky really bigger in Montana—and if so, why?

—Florence Johns, Denver, Colorado

A We called the Montana travel office and got Lana on the line. "Maybe because the state is so spread out?" she said. "Or because the population is low?" Stand on Montana's high prairies and there are no telephone poles, skyscrapers, liquor billboards, or water slides to muck up the vista. Montana has little pollution and low humidity, which makes for less haze, fewer clouds, and a razor-sharp horizon. You actually see more of the sky.

But wait—what about the rest of the West? Can Montana truly lay claim to the "Big Sky" appellation? What about, say, Wyoming, which has about three hundred thousand fewer people than Montana blocking the celestial view? When we called the tourism office in Cheyenne and asked if the residents of the Equality State didn't think their sky might be just as big, or perhaps even a little bigger, an unruffled spokeswoman clucked definitively, "Oh, I would think so."

Q What are the most dangerous volcanoes around the world today?

—Dylan Warner, Ketchum, Idaho

A Topping volcanologists' A-list is Popocatepetl, a 17,887-foot peak that's been spewing ash on Mexico City since 1992. Scientists fear that even a minor eruption could melt the snow on Popo's flanks and create a massive, fast-moving mud surge, known as a *lahar,* that could overrun the large communities along its drainages. (A lahar from Colombia's Nevado del Ruiz volcano buried some twenty-three thousand people alive in 1985.) Experts also fear an encore from Italy's legendary Vesuvius, the source of recent rumblings and not a few nights of lost sleep in nearby Naples. Closer to home, the rock interior of Washington's Mount Rainier has been so hollowed out by erosion that a small tremor could cause the steep slopes to cave in on themselves, unleashing a devastating lahar. Says Ed Klimasauskas, of the

U.S. Geological Survey's Cascades Volcano Observatory, "We're worried that Rainier may be rotting from the inside out." Even more worrisome, however, is the ever-energetic Mount St. Helens, whose steam blasts of late have prompted a few bold researchers to predict a major eruption in the next several years. But volcanology is a notoriously inexact science, so don't hold your breath.

Q It seems like the world's big continental "points"—like Cape Horn—all aim south. Is this significant?
—Troy Kitch, Guam

A You mean, did the continents long ago all melt and "drip" southward? Not at all. Geologists believe that Africa, South America, and India were all part of a megacontinent, which they call Gondwanaland, that fragmented millions of years ago. Africa and South America in particular have a similarly pointy aspect because they broke off Gondwanaland like two slices of the same pie. "If you drop a plate on the floor," says University of Texas geophysicist Lawrence Lawver, "you'll get some pointy pieces and some square pieces." That's what happened when Gondwanaland broke up. At the moment a lot of its pointy shards happen to be aimed south. In a billion years, they'll be pointing somewhere else. Geology is so fleeting.

Q Did they ever learn why that African lake belched up poison gas back in the 1980s? Is it safe to return?

—A. J. Johnson, Boston, Massachusetts

A On August 21, 1986, Cameroon's Lake Nyos emitted a giant cloud of carbon dioxide that killed more than 1,700 people within a fifteen-mile radius. Survivors thought they'd been hit by a neutron bomb. This wasn't the region's first such disaster—nearby Lake Monoun let loose in 1984, killing thirty-seven—and it won't be the last: Nyos could blow again at any time, with even more catastrophic results. University of Michigan lake expert George Kling worries that the next eruption of Nyos could collapse a feeble natural dam at one end of the lake, which he says could cause one of the worst floods in history, as the countryside below is heavily populated. Both Nyos and Monoun are deep, stagnant, acutely stratified volcanic lakes fed by carbonated springs. Over time they build up an enormous charge of carbon dioxide, which can burst to the surface if the lake is disturbed by, say, a landslide or volcanic activity. As of this writing, officials in Cameroon are examining a plan to "defizz" Nyos and Monoun by pumping out the CO_2 through a network of pipes; the only trick will be to slip the pipes in carefully enough to avoid setting off another killer cloud.

Q Recently I spotted a continental divide sign in the middle of North Dakota, on a flat stretch of 194, near Jamestown. What's going on here?

—Peter Salter, Mandan, North Dakota

A That sign isn't a hoax, but it has nothing to do with *the* continental divide, the one that runs down the spine of the Rockies and separates rivers that flow into the Pacific from those that empty into the Gulf of Mexico. The divide you stumbled on is a broad, swampy zone that starts up in Saskatchewan and runs across North Dakota, separating rivers that flow south toward the Gulf of Mexico from rivers that flow north and east into Hudson Bay. Call it the Northern Divide, if you want. But is this a true continental divide? Hard to say. Geographers point out that the Appalachian chain, which is sometimes called the Eastern Divide, isn't a divide at all, as the waters on both sides ultimately empty into the Atlantic Ocean (because the Gulf of Mexico is technically the Atlantic). But some experts are willing to concede that this Northern Divide of yours might be a little different, as Hudson Bay is generally considered part of the Arctic Ocean. Still, you want to be conservative in these matters. Once you start creating new divides, cautions a spokesman at the U.S. Geological Survey, "You could just go on ad infinitum." And the country seems divided enough already.

earthistentialism

Q I've heard that the magenetic North Pole is moving! Is my 1950 compass out-of-date?

—Mel Saltaine, Ojai, California

A The more we learn about the capricious doings of our planet, the more we discover that those concepts we revere for their sense of permanence and order are only shadowy readings of a world in flux. This is especially true of the earth's geomagnetic field, which, far from being a constant or uniform force that blankets us all, can be a wildly idiosyncratic thing. Yes, it's true that magnetic north is shifting, not only from year to year, but even from day to day, and this is a consequence of the perpetual glurping and sloshing around of the molten iron in the liquid core of the earth. Magnetic north, of course, is the N to which our compasses point. It's not exactly a location, with precise coordinates, but rather a broad region of magnetic concentration, the master terminal of what is essentially a giant bar magnet. As of this writing, magnetic north can be found at latitude 80.95 degrees north and longitude 110.10 degrees west, which puts it in the general location of Canada's Sverdrup Islands. Scientists at the U.S. Geological Survey (USGS) who track its migration tell us that magnetic north has been gadding about the Arctic Circle for some 750,000 years, at one point straying as far as thirty degrees southward, about the equivalent of Anchorage.

What's even weirder than magnetic north's wanderlust, and somehow more unsettling, is that every five hundred thousand years or so, our entire magnetic field undergoes a complete "flip." That is, the whole world turns upside down; magnetic north becomes magnetic south, and vice versa. Some prognosticators have predicted that the next reversal will occur about two thousand years from now, and have speculated on the various hells that will break loose when it does, including the profound navigational confusion that will be suffered by those birds, fish, and other creatures that depend on the earth's magnetic field to get their bearings.

That's still a ways off, but those of us living in the here and now have, as you rightly suggest, a more practical problem to deal with: namely, what about our compasses? First of all, don't fret; your 1950 model is as accurate as any other. It points to magnetic north just as faithfully as a brand-new one will. What you have to worry about is not your old compass but rather your old maps. All good maps are oriented toward true north, and they make allowances for *declination,* the discrepancy between true and magnetic north, by including precise calculations that enable you to adjust your compass heading. Depending on where you are in the world at any given time, this discrepancy can be significant, and if you happen to be working off an old map from, say, 1950, the declination figures will be way, way off, enough so that if you're doing any nip-and-tuck navigating, you might get yourself seriously lost. This is the reason why the USGS updates its maps every five years—and why, before heading out into the wilderness, you should always check the vintage of your map. (By the way, most handheld GPS devices are programmed to adjust automatically to the whimsical nature of magnetic north.)

One further thought to compound our sense of living a thoroughly untethered existence: We might countenance the wanderings of magnetic north, but at least "true" north never budges, right? Well, yes and no. True north might be a fixed point—one whose whereabouts, using the stars and a complicated series of calculations, is possible to pinpoint down to the millimeter—but it's far from being a fixed piece of real estate. If you were to pitch camp on the North Pole tonight, by morning you would no longer be there, because the ice floes under which the pole invisibly resides are ceaselessly drifting to and fro in the Arctic Ocean. An explorer's flag or any other man-made demarcation would assume a pitiful evanescence. And so the search for absolutes continues.

Q Say I'm out sailing in the ocean and there's another boat on the horizon. Under ideal circum- stances, at what point does that boat "disappear" behind the planet's curvature?

—*Curry Haley, Houston, Texas*

A Visibility on the high seas is rarely optimal, thanks to the atmosphere's consistently high humidity and the salty particulate matter ceaselessly churned up in ocean spray. But if you're close to the water's surface, as your question presupposes, the curvature of the earth should kick in well before this briny scuzz washes out your vista. For a six-foot-tall person standing at sea level, the great planetary bend is only about three miles away. If this sounds astonishingly close, bear in mind this basic principle: When it comes to the earth's curvature, altitude is everything. The higher you are, the more extended the horizon. Shinny thirty feet up your mast, and you'll extend your range to seven miles; jump overboard, and your visual range will shrink to less than a mile. The height of the distant boat is equally important: a hulking oil tanker will ride high above the horizon, visible from perhaps twenty miles away, long before it mows you down.

But let's turn things around. Let's say you're in a sailboat, gazing back toward shore at a massive mountain range looming in the far distance. Let's also say that the air over the landmass is exquisitely clean and dry, affording what pilots call *cavu* (ceiling and visibility unlimited) conditions. From how far away can you see these peaks before they start hazing out? "The naked eye can make out something big—like a mountain range—as long as there is more than a 2 percent contrast between that object and the sky," notes physicist William Malm, a visibility expert with the National Park Service. "In absolutely particulate-free air, you might be able to see mountains as far away as 240 miles." But that would be the extreme outer limit; anything beyond that, Malm says, and the intervening atmosphere will scatter the light enough to nudge the contrast below the 2 percent threshold. The mountains will still be there, but no one, not even Barbra Streisand, can see them.

Q Earth's core is constantly losing heat, right? Shouldn't we be worried about global cooling?

—Karen Erlandson, Goleta, California

A Actually, Earth is far from becoming the third snowball from the Sun, even though we are perpetually spinning in the subfreezing meatlocker of space. The core got hot about 4.5 billion years ago, when our vulnerable planet is believed to have collided with another planet-size body. The core temperature was approximately twelve thousand degrees Fahrenheit then, and it's dropped by only about a thousand degrees since. At present cooling rates, the core should be toasty for tens of billions of years. Besides, geological heat doesn't contribute much to the total planetary energy picture above ground: scientists measure the internal heat energy radiated at the earth's surface in milliwatts per square meter, and a football-field-size parcel gives off only about two hundred watts—barely enough to power a couple of lightbulbs.

It's also true that various radioactive elements inside the earth are producing new heat all the time. The oven, in other words, is still turned "on." But the main reason the core has stayed hot, according to University of California, Berkeley, geophysicist Raymond Jeanloz, is that rock is a terrific insulator. "Even if you could instantly turn off the core heat, we wouldn't know it for millions of years," he says. "We'd have volcanoes and earthquakes for a long time to come."

Q If the topsoil is perpetually sloughing off and blowing away— as environmental doomsayers tell us—why do archaeologists dig deeper into the earth to find older civilizations?

—Rafael Domingo, El Paso, Texas

A The erosion and deposition of sedimentary dust is the great, silent yin-and-yang of earth science. While it's true that topsoil and rock everywhere are steadily slough-ing off and kicking up fine particles of dirt into the atmos-phere, that same dirt is just as steadily coming down somewhere else. It's a zero-sum game of global scope: One region's loss of sediment is another's gain. "The Buddhists had it right all along," notes the dean of Mesoamerican archaeology, Yale's Michael D. Coe. "Everything is in con-tinuous motion. Mountains are being worn down, but new mountains are being formed. Sediment is dumping into rivers, but those same rivers are dumping it on the banks somewhere downstream. And no matter how hard you scrub away the wind-blown dirt, it just keeps raining down on you."

As you bear this overarching principle in mind, under-stand that archaeologists don't always dig deeper to find older things. Changing weather patterns and a host of other factors can cause whole civilizations to pop up in impressive ways. Along the ancient Silk Route of Central Asia, for example, stout Mongolian winds have caused extensive cities (such as the 1,500-year-old Kingdom of Loulan ruins) to rise like phantoms from the ground in recent years. In general, places that happen to be situated down in valleys (such as Rome's Tiber River Valley, to take one locality of particular archaeological import) tend to accumulate more of this universal dust than do places located along the flanks of mountains, which are usually more exposed to wind and subject to steeper, swifter drainage.

One reason archaeologists are so often digging *down* to find the ancient stuff has to do with another factor altogether: Cities create their own forms of dust over time, dust caused by the discarding of everyday trash and the weathering of the buildings themselves, particularly if they're made out of soft, crumbly substances like mud. Thus, when humans have been living in a particular site for a long, long time—like, say, in Damascus, Syria— archaeologists often find layer cakes of civilization, known as *tells,* which are the result of generation after generation of people giving up on their decrepit dwellings and starting again atop old foundations.

Even in a place where the sedimentary stratification does generally follow the deeper-is-older paradigm, any number of localized quirks can disturb the tidy layer pattern in the soil. Earthquakes, floods, streams that change course over time, even burrowing rodents and insects— any of these factors can move around the archaeological furniture to such an extent that the depth at which a given relic is discovered might not offer the faintest clue as to its age. More compelling proof, as if we needed it, that there's no such thing as terra firma.

Q What's the maximum number of people Earth can hold?

—*Andrew Ciancaglini, Denver, Colorado*

A In 1999 our fair planet arrived at an alarming benchmark. According to the United Nations, sometime in mid-October, a child was born somewhere in the world, and global population officially reached six billion *homo sapiens.* If that doesn't plunge you into a Malthusian funk, consider that at present population growth rates, the world will be home to 694 billion humans by the year 2150. You don't have to be a "deep ecology" hairshirt to wonder: Can the planet *stand* that many people? Is there enough soil, water, and air to keep 694 billion human hearts beating? The best guess is, probably not. Of course, the Cassandras have been wrong before, and many optimists maintain that human ingenuity can arrest these trends and solve the attendant environmental problems as they arise. But in recent years demographers and environmentalists have turned their attention with an increasing sense of alarm to the question of our planet's maximum occupancy or *carrying capacity,* as it's usually called. Though it's a nearly impossible number to divine, the median estimates range anywhere from 7.7 billion to 12 billion people—figures we should easily reach within the present century. And then what? Does the planet slip from its orbit? Does it collapse under its own demographic weight? Does everything . . . stop? Doomsayers have warned about a coming "demographic winter," when our population spirals will be corrected by massive viral epidemics, wars, or environmental catastrophes on a scale never seen before. But most likely all that will happen is that life will become increasingly miserable for all of us: bad air, bad water, bad food, and less of it. The apocalypse won't be apocalyptic, it will come in shabby little increments, against the backdrop of an ever more toxic and more attenuated ecosphere. Take Cairo or Manila on a bad day, and that will be the human condition. "What's the planet's carrying capacity?" writes Rockefeller University demographer Joel Cohen, author of *How Many People Can the Earth Support?* "The fact is that no single number exists. It's a trick question, because the answer really depends on what people want out of life."

Q As Earth spins, what kinds of matter leak out into the universe?

—Frank DePaul, Las Vegas, Nevada

A We are not residents of a hermetically sealed ball. You'd be surprised how much stuff we leave behind, whether accidentally, incidentally, or on purpose. For starters, gases such as helium, hydrogen, oxygen, and nitrogen are constantly defying gravity and escaping from our upper ionosphere, swept away by solar winds. Then, of course, there are light waves—infrared light, reflected sunlight, and the luminance of major metropolises—which are flung into space at a fleet 186,000 miles per second. As for more tangible castoffs, the U.S. and Russian space programs have sent a total of sixty-five probes to other planets and beyond—including the *Voyager 1* spacecraft that's currently hurtling out of our solar system carrying a disc of greetings in fifty-five languages, plus recordings of humpback whale calls, Mozart sonatas, and Chuck Berry's "Johnny B. Goode." Earthlings have made at least one other notable attempt to leave our imprimatur on the cosmos: In 1974 scientists beamed a potent, three-minute electronic signal from the half-million-watt transmitter at Puerto Rico's Arecibo Radio Observatory. "It was undoubtedly the strongest deliberate message that we've ever sent—easily strong enough to be heard on the far side of the galaxy," says California-based astronomer Seth Shostak with the organization SETI. Arguably our most indelible imprints on the universe, however, are the millions of hours of FM radio and television transmissions that have been inadvertently seeping heavenward for the better part of the last century. "The first TV broadcasts are approximately 240 trillion miles away from us now," says Shostak. "They have washed over some two thousand stars, any of which could theoretically have a planet with intelligent life. Right now there are worlds out there that may be tuning into episodes of *Mister Ed*—and really wondering."

h2-oh!

Fluid thoughts on the nature of water

Q Why are oceans salty?
—Lucy Wood, Nairobi, Kenya

A When rainwater falls on the ground, much of it drains via creeks and rivers toward the sea. Along the way, it picks up salts from the rocks and soil. Thus rivers become progressively saltier as they head downstream. For example, by the time the Mississippi River nears the Gulf of Mexico, its salt content has swelled to about two parts per thousand. All of these salts are dumped in the ocean. And here's the trick: When seawater evaporates, the salt stays behind. Some ends up in sediment on the ocean floor. The rest stays in solution and gives surfers perfect complexions.

Why aren't lakes salty? Because most of them drain. But landlocked lakes, especially in hot, dry climates, can get extremely briny. The Great Salt Lake clocks in at 240 parts per thousand, compared to only 35 ppt for the oceans. Although the whole rain-and-drain process has been going on ever since there were oceans, we're in no danger of a terrestrial salt shortage: there should be enough in the ground (sodium being the seventh most common substance in the earth's crust) to keep the cycle going another billion years.

Q Why does water come in so many shades of blue?

—Paul Hohenleitner, Langhorne, Pennsylvania

A "Water transmits and scatters blue better than any other color," notes physicist Howard R. Gordon of the University of Miami, Coral Gables. Translation: As it passes deeper into the ocean, sunlight grows progressively bluer as other colors in the spectrum are absorbed. In general, deep, clear water looks the bluest, especially under a bright blue sky. If you have shallow water over a sandy bottom, it'll reflect white and green light, giving you an azure color. In overcast weather, the sea will turn a slate blue, the result of the reflection of clouds on the surface. Finally, phytoplankton suspended in water will give it a greenish blue hue.

Where is the bluest ocean water, in the opinion of a professional? "The Sargasso Sea in the Atlantic Ocean," Gordon says. "It has the richest blue on the planet, with less pollution and less phytoplankton than anywhere. And it's about four miles deep."

Q Can a sailboat go faster than the wind?

—Andrew Newcomb, Andover, Massachusetts

A Yes, but you probably can't afford it. Under ideal conditions, certain extremely light multihull sailboats benefit from a phenomenon called *apparent wind*—the true wind combined with the wind that comes over the bow as you move forward. All sailboats experience apparent wind, but any gain on wind speed is usually checked by the drag of the hull. Boats that routinely outsail the wind are rare because they're extremely expensive and uncomfortable, the esoteric trimaran designs of speed-obsessed engineers. (By the way, it should also be noted that elite windsurfers routinely go faster than the wind, but that's another story.) The world speed record for sailing—46.52 knots, or 53.57 miles per hour—was set by one of these exotic multihulled vessels sailing off the coast of Australia in 1993. By comparison, the most impressive speed ever clocked by an America's Cup yacht was a relatively languorous 22 knots.

Q Officially, what is it that distinguishes a river from a creek?

—Bill Jorns, Tokyo, Japan

A The problem is worse than you think. The U.S. Board on Geographic Names, which is the court of last resort on such matters, has recorded 154 different terms for what it calls a "linear, overland, flowing body of water." So we don't just have rivers and creeks to contend with; we have ances, bournes, cams, drokes, freshets, guzzles, kills . . . on and on it goes. Some of them are quite specific. An *anabranch,* for instance, is a bit of river that veers from the main course and then returns to it later. Others are impossible to nail down: A *bogue* is a swamp in some parts of the country and a stream in others; a *coulee* in Louisiana is filled with water, whereas in Montana it's usually dry. Basically, there is no precise, consistent, nationally applicable definition of a river or creek. The board's solution? It simply refers to all linear, overland, flowing bodies of water as *streams,* and leaves it at that.

It's much the same thing with lakes versus ponds. The U.S. Board on Geographic Names refers to all "natural bodies of inland water" with the generic term *lake.* But we don't live in a generic world, and in deference to that happy fact, the board recognizes fifty-four different varieties of lakes. Among the more obscure entries on the list are the *charco,* an intermittent pool found in Oregon and Texas; Utah's *guzzler,* a flooded area close to a stream; and Central Park's northernmost body of water, the Meer. Ultimately, the difference between a lake and a pond is in the eye of the original namer. "It's a very subjective and emotional process," says board executive secretary Roger Payne, who is quick to add that there are ninety-five federally recognized Big Ponds and 1,366 Little Lakes in this country. "We're not here to question people's logic."

Q How many times can a stone skip on water?

—Adrian McCloskey, Rapid City, South Dakota

A Virtually every culture has a term for stone skipping. The English call it *ducks and drakes*; to Danes, it's *smutting*. Eskimos skip rocks on ice, Bedouins on smooth sand. Currently, The *Guinness Book of World Records* accords the title to Jerdone Coleman McGhee, a Texas engineer who in 1992 scored (and videotaped) an incredible thirty-eight skips on the Blanco River. Author of *The Secrets of Stone Skipping,* McGhee has consulted with MIT engineering students, who've used strobe photography to analyze the fluid dynamics of a skip (which, by the way, involves releasing the stone almost parallel to the water, with enough velocity and spin to create a small wave on impact and then bounce off that wave and go airborne again). McGhee's mark is not without controversy, however. Purists insist that skipping prowess undergoes its true test only in a sanctioned competition, when the heat is on. The granddaddy of all such skip-offs is held every Fourth of July on Michigan's Mackinac Island. It was here in 1975 that John Kolar earned the all-time Mackinac record of "twenty-four-plus-infinity" (his stone vanished ominously into fog after two dozen skips). Kolar calls Mackinac, with its variable weather, disruptive boat traffic, and nearly constant chop, the "Wimbledon Centre Court of skipping—it quickly weeds out the competition." Indeed, when Jerdone McGhee made the pilgrimage to Mackinac, he was duly humbled by a score of only seventeen.

Q Is there really such a thing as sea level? Isn't the "level" always changing with the tides and melting icebergs and other stuff?

—Ron Sterns, Boise, Idaho

A Nothing in our world, not even sea level, is absolute. "Sea level is a hard value to pin down, because it varies a lot around the world due to tides, seasons, and other factors," says Steve Gill of the National Ocean Service. Most of the time, when you hear people talking about sea level, they're referring to some variation on *mean sea level,* an average that's based on hourly measurements of water levels taken at various stations around the world. Scientists agree that sea level is currently rising at a rate of about a millimeter and a half per year, a calculation that factors in a whole raft of geophysical variables. For instance, around Galveston, Texas, sea level appears to be rising faster than the global rate because the land there is subsiding, a result of oil extraction, among other things. In other places, such as the coast of southern Alaska, sea level appears to be falling, because the retreat of heavy glaciers is causing the landmass to rise imperceptibly.

So which sea-level standard are the elevation figures found in maps based upon? Many surveyors are still working off something called the *National Geodetic Verti-*

cal Datum (NGVD), a sort of zero point that was calculated way back in 1929. You'd think we were due for a new fixed point in our lives, and we are: Though some cartographers have been slow to embrace the new reality, the NGVD has now been officially replaced by the more accurate *North American Vertical Datum*, based on 1988 data. Eventually all new maps will work off the new elevation figures. When they do, the odds are, you're going to come down in the world.

Q I've heard that scuba diving is really bad for your bones. Should I find a new sport?

—*Angus Miller, Spokane, Washington*

A The average scuba enthusiast has little to worry about, but commercial divers who make frequent descents of more than 100 feet have been known to suffer from a crippling affliction known as *dysbaric osteonecrosis*—or, more ominously, *bone death*. It's a degenerative condition that can make bones dangerously brittle and cause excruciating pain in the joints. Veteran scallop and urchin divers or frogman mechanics who service oil rigs seem to be particularly susceptible to osteonecrosis over the long haul. Though the science behind the malady isn't yet fully understood, here's what we do know: Under pressure, nitrogen is squeezed out of the bloodstream into the surrounding tissues. When a diver rises slowly, the nitrogen is reabsorbed gradually into the blood. Should he ascend too quickly, however, gas bubbles will linger in the tissues, blocking the flow of blood to the bones and resulting in a painful, perhaps fatal, case of the bends. But that's just the short term. Osteonecrosis occurs after lengthy exposure to great depths, when areas of the bone—especially around the knees, shoulders, and hips—start to weaken from lack of blood. Little lesions and spiny spurs begin to form on the bones, and if not allowed to mend, bone tissues start to die off. Unless the person stops diving altogether, the bone will become prone to chipping or breaking or, in the most extreme cases, will degenerate into severe arthritis, with joint-replacement often being the only viable treatment. Such is the fate of 20 percent of Maine's commercial scallop divers, a sad and hobbled class of retirees who make Joe Namath look spry.

Q If a laptop computer or any electrical item were to fall into a large body of water, how far would the electric current travel?

—M. Mroczkowski, Sacramento, California

A Because the mission of an electric current is to find the shortest and easiest route to the ground—be it through a wooden pier, a nearby wader, or a submerged aluminum pipe—it will travel only as far as it has to, which in water is usually no more than fifty feet. Whether the current would actually leave its wire circuit and enter the water, however, depends on a host of particular circumstances.

Here are a few points to consider in such a scenario. First, is the appliance battery operated? If so, then you have no worries at all. The waterlogged item would simply short-circuit itself, without dangerous electrical fanfare. If it's plugged in, however, you might be in serious trouble (in fact, you might already be dead, in which case there's no need to read on), especially if you're in salt water, which is rife with voltage-loving ions and thus conducts electricity significantly better than freshwater. The presence of carbon dioxide also can boost conductivity, thus making a muddy pond filled with rotting stumps and other carbon-rich detritus more attractive to a live wire than, say, a clean, deep, granite quarry. Whatever you do, you want to make sure of two things: First, that you're not directly touching the appliance in question. Second, that your feet are not touching the bottom, thus creating a ground for the current and turning your body into the next best thing to copper wiring. You want to float on the water's surface and swim directly away from the offending object. Probably the best approach is proactive, however: next time you head for a swimming hole, just leave the laptop at home.

Q I've heard that the Pacific Ocean's sea level is higher than the Atlantic's. How can this be?

—John Frederick, New York, New York

A Strange as it sounds, it's true. Not only is the Pacific Ocean about twice the size of the Atlantic, but it's also, on average, twenty centimeters higher. To an islander in the South Pacific, this can mean the difference between a flooded cabana and a dry bed. Remember that sea level isn't an absolute, but merely an average of the changes in ocean level over time—as determined by a bunch of different variables, such as currents, wind, and tides. Most significant, however, is salinity. Due to generally higher evaporative rates overall, the Atlantic is saltier, denser, and thus slightly lower than the Pacific. As for what occurs at *transitional* zones such as off Cape Horn, where the Pacific and Atlantic collide, there's not much to see. The twenty-centimeter discrepancy, after all, is based upon measurements taken over some ninety-five million square miles of ocean. Columbia University oceanographer Arnold Gordon puts it this way: "If you're on a boat passing from the Atlantic to the Pacific, it won't exactly feel like you're going uphill."

Q Why does my husband's wet suit have such a horrible smell? It's unnatural!

—C. P., Houston, Texas

A You couldn't design a better habitat for odoriferous microorganisms than a neoprene wet suit. Look at a cross section of the rubbery fabric and you'll see the problem: Neoprene, expressly designed to be porous, is honeycombed with thousands of tiny air-filled tunnels, any one of which makes a perfect niche for colonies of microscopic critters that float around in oceans and lakes. Vibrio bacteria, diotoms, and algae are usually the principal offenders. Once they attach to your wet suit, these microbial invaders burrow into the darkest, wettest interstices and begin growing and feeding off nutrients provided by your own body: carotene from your sloughing skin cells, salts from your sweat, fats from your body oils, and even nitrogen from your urine. (We're not pointing any fingers, but it happens.) "A wet suit offers bacteria and algae a giant smorgasbord," explains American Society of Microbiology president Jay Grimes (yes, his real name). "With so much stuff for them to feast on, you get a nice community growing in there in no time." In a matter of hours, a complex food chain develops, with various forms of mildew soon joining the party. The final ingredients for wetsuit fetor are prolonged darkness and heat. Leave a drenched wet suit (one that has neither been rinsed in neoprene-friendly disinfectant nor hung out to dry) in a sun-baked trunk for a week, and you'll not only need a new Body-Glove, you'll want a new car.

up on the roof

high concepts about mountains

Q I've heard that Ecuador's Mount Chimborazo is higher than Everest. Am I missing something?

—Roberta Jones, Anchorage, Alaska

A Though cartographers strictly measure a mountain's height above mean sea level, some people get caught up in more esoteric definitions, such as the distance between a mountain's summit and its base. By this yardstick, Hawaii's Mauna Kea volcano, whose 13,796-foot summit rises about 46,600 feet from its base on the seafloor, is significantly taller than Everest. Chimborazo poses a third definitional subtlety. First you need to understand that the earth isn't perfectly round; the equator bulges 13.3 miles farther out into space than the poles do. Hence the base of a mountain near the equator is actually farther from the center of the planet than the base of a mountain elsewhere. Chimborazo rises to 20,561 feet, which makes it the world's 99th-tallest mountain by standard measure, underwhelming to say the least. But because it's located just one hundred miles south of the equator, Chimborazo beats the Himalayan peak hands down if you're an adherent of the "bulge" criterion.

So are world-class mountaineers forsaking Everest in droves to go conquer Chimborazo? "No," says David Doyle, senior scientist at the National Geodetic Survey. "You don't start climbing a mountain from the center of the earth—not unless you're Jules Verne."

Q What's alpenglow? Is it a scientific phenomenon, or a poetic term?

—*Jackson Mayer, Medford, Oregon*

A *Alpenglow* has a vaguely medieval ring to it, but the word was actually coined in 1871. It comes from the German *alpen,* "mountain," and *glute,* "fire," and describes the brilliant rosy light that you find when a sunrise or sunset reflects on a mountain peak. It can make for a stunning après-ski effect to be sitting down in a dark valley, where the sunset has long since disappeared from view, while the west-facing crags above are ablaze with reds and pinks.

Alpenglow is most striking on snow-covered peaks, where all that white only intensifies the fiery hues. People who live in big cities with skyscrapers can enjoy a special variation on the theme. In Chicago, for example, the phenomenon is officially known as Searstowerglow. Urban dwellers have found that plate glass has a poetry all its own.

Q I live at sea level, and when I go climbing in Colorado I get nosebleeds. Why?

—Linda Flegel, Vancouver, British Columbia, Canada

A A variety of factors conspire to make mountains a bane to nasal cavities. Everyone knows that high-altitude air is extremely dry (thin, cold, low-pressure air holds less moisture), but the subtleties of the schnozz are more complicated: "The skin inside your nose isn't like the skin on your arms and legs," says Dr. Murray Grossan, a Los Angeles ear, nose, and throat specialist. "It's paper-thin and loaded with blood vessels." A few hours in the mountains, and the dry, oxygen-lean air will transform your nasal tissue into a chapped and bleeding mess. Humidifiers and saline spray can help, but if the problem lingers, consider consulting your doctor. Says Dr. Grossan: "A person who bleeds repeatedly and profusely at higher altitudes may be suffering from something more serious, like a deviated septum—or a cocaine problem."

Q How do mogul fields form?

—Kathleen Randall, New York, New York

A Think of a mogul field as an elaborate public-works project created and continually revised by the skiing masses. To make a nice one you need two basic ingredients: lots of powdery snow and lots of skiers, preferably expert skiers, fluidly linking thousands upon thousands of tight S-turns down the fall line of a slope. Remember that when you're skiing, you're not just leaving a discreet set of tracks in the snow; you're actually pushing the stuff around, sculpting it and leaving little slag piles with every turn. Multiply your actions by those of legions of other skiers, and the whole slope becomes a vast rococo of grooves and ridges. Subsequent skiers then react to these emerging developments. Because most people tend to negotiate the same terrain in predictable ways, turning on the crest of the ridge and sliding into the trough, they gradually accentuate these patterns: the grooves become deeper, the bumps become higher. As long as the slope isn't groomed, a mogul field will take shape, with the floor plan subtly changing from day to day. A mogul run can abide spontaneity and individualism, but only so much: Those nice uniform humps are the cumulative results of each skier's respecting the general rhythms laid down by his predecessor. Fishtailing snowboarders (not that we're judging!) tend to muck up those clean lines, as do tentative skiers who make disruptive side cuts into the mountain. The exacting mogul fields used in World Cup freestyle competitions are made the same way as all others, only with a little more scientific precision: Officials plant bamboo poles every ten feet down a virgin slope, and then have test skiers go to work, run after run after run, chiseling out a perfectionist's gauntlet of snowy Bubble Wrap.

Q If hot air rises, why is it always cooler in the mountains?

—William Conway, Louisville, Kentucky

A Hot air rises, but it doesn't *stay* hot. On its way sky-ward, decreasing atmospheric pressure causes it to expand and, consequently, gradually grow colder in a process called *adiabatic cooling*. Eventually, the formerly hot air becomes so chilly that it stops rising altogether.

We all know now that the Greek myth of Daedalus and Icarus got it exactly backward: It's cooler in the higher altitudes. This is because air is warmed for the most part by sunlight hitting the surface of the earth. The farther you get from the radiant effects of the ground, the lower the temperature—about 3.6 degrees Fahrenheit lower for every thousand feet of ascent. (Of course, mountains are "the ground," too, but whereas sunlight warms peaks just as it warms valleys, mountains are surrounded by brisk, breezy, high-altitude air, which keeps them refrigerated.) All things being equal, the summit of Mount Everest ought to be an invigorating 104 degrees cooler than sea level.

By the way, hot air doesn't always rise. Anyone who's spent a summer in, say, Washington, D.C., knows that under certain atmospheric conditions, hot air can just lie around for weeks at a time, slow-cooking the citizens and making them yearn for the mountains.

up there

nature's ticked!

shocking truths from the meteorological vault

Q How big can a hailstone get?
—*Claire Marshall, Park City, Utah*

A Big. Disturbingly, outlandishly, lethally big. Hailstones—such as the "cricket ball"-size ones that killed 250 people and some 1,600 sheep and goats in India in 1888—are born deep inside the gusty green turbulence of cumulonimbus thunderclouds. In such storms, powerful updrafts of more than one hundred miles per hour can suck raindrops as high as eleven miles into the sky, quickly turning them into ice crystals. These crystals collide into one another to form tiny pebbles of hail that can make numerous trips down and back up again to the upper

reaches of the storm cloud. As it accrues one onionlike layer of ice after another, the stone will eventually become so immense that the updrafts can no longer support it, and it plummets to the ground. What's the most humongous hailstone found to date? There are several leading candidates. An icy rock weighing seven-and-a-half pounds fell on Hyderabad, India, on March 17, 1939, but it was never officially authenticated and, in any case, it's believed to have been an amalgam of numerous stones frozen together. In March of 1982, a thirty-pound chunk of ice left a large divot in a hill near Tecumseh, Oklahoma, but in a rather unsettling denouement, investigators determined that it was probably "blue ice" from an airliner's leaky lavatory that had built up on the fuselage before shearing off and falling to the ground.

The National Oceanic and Atmospheric Administration (NOAA) gives the official prize to the 1.75-pound basketball-size bomb that fell near the home of Dan White in Coffeyville, Kansas, in September 1970. "I hope I never see anything like that again," says White, noting that NOAA meteorologists made a plaster cast of the spiky orb—now displayed at the Dalton Defenders Museum in downtown Coffeyville. "I seen this green wall cloud coming, and I said, 'We're going to get some hail out of that!' The boys went out with buckets to hunt for hailstones. It's a good thing they were wearing their football helmets— they would have been knocked lulu!"

Q In the Midwest, forecasters are always blaming blizzards on the "lake effect." Are they for real, or are weathermen just trying to pass the buck?

—Jason O'Brian, Grand Rapids, Michigan

A Rest assured that lake effect is not some kind of meteorological conspiracy. It's completely legitimate; in fact, it's a global phenomenon—Russia's Lake Baikal is a notorious blizzard factory. Nowhere, however, is it stronger than in the Great Lakes region, where topographic and atmospheric conditions provide an ideal birthing ground for monster storms. It happens like this: A stiff, cold breeze sweeps for many miles over a large body of water, causing cloudlets of ice crystals to evaporate like steam off the lake's surface. (The size of the lake is crucial. Lake Superior certainly has the necessary square mileage and then some, whereas Lake Champlain, declared a "great" lake by delusional New York promoters a few years back, does not.) When the arctic winds fetch themselves to shore, these clouds—now saturated with humidity—are forced upward into chillier realms. And because cold air holds less moisture, the bottom literally drops out. When it does, you can expect ludicrous amounts of snow; sometimes as much as four feet can fall during a single day, with almost all of it occurring as a localized event in distinct bands just a few miles inland from the lake. Given the prevailing weather patterns, it's usually the *eastern* shores of the Great Lakes that see the brunt. Marquette,

Michigan, is the unrivaled lake-effect capital of the world, a town inauspiciously situated on the Upper Peninsula in the crosshairs of both Lake Superior and Lake Michigan. Average annual snow dumpage: 121 inches.

Q Why is Bangladesh continually clobbered by natural calamities?

—Cass Tomlin, Butler, Pennsylvania

A Low-lying Bangladesh is situated at the head of the Bay of Bengal, a spawning ground for typhoons and tornadoes, not to mention the occasional roving tsunami, and the country lies in the floodplain of the Ganges, Brahmaputra, and Meghna Rivers, which swell every spring with Himalayan snowmelt. Add to this mix an intense monsoon season and a population density of more than 2,100 people per square mile, and you have an ongoing formula for natural disasters—like 1991's Typhoon Walt, which lashed Bangladesh with 143-mile-per-hour winds and twenty-foot waves, killing 138,000 people. Year after year, it's a grim illustration of the adage, "geography is destiny."

Q What is heat lightning?

—Russ Sauvageau, Ocala, Florida

A Sometimes mistakenly regarded as an exotic sub-species of lightning—a bolt from Zeus's reserve quiver—*heat lightning* is actually just a colloquialism for any kind of atmospheric electricity that's too far away to be heard. It's lightning without thunder, in other words. On hot summer evenings, particularly in wide-open country that permits unobstructed vistas, heat lightning appears as the flickerings of a storm that can be as far as one hundred miles away. Instead of seeing distinct lightning bolts, you often get a diffuse luminance, as though a strobe is flashing in the murkiest recesses of a very distant cloud. Since thunder's sound waves ordinarily can travel no more than fifteen miles, heat lightning seems to be silent—a muzzled light show with an especially eerie beauty. Sometimes storms, like children, should be seen and not heard.

Q "Red sky by night, sailor's delight. Red sky by morning, sailor take warning." Is it true?

—Paul Johnican, Des Moines, Iowa

A Variations of this ancient saying turn up in Shakespeare and even in the Gospel of Matthew. Some meteorologists have estimated that the "night" part of the proverb can be as much as 70 percent accurate in forecasting rain—not bad, as folk wisdom goes, but not good enough to drive the Weather Channel off the air.

There's no consensus on why it works as well as it does, but here's the basic concept: Sunlight comes to us through more miles of the atmosphere at dawn and dusk than at other times of day. When the sky is clear, the atmosphere scatters the light at the blue end of the spectrum, leaving mostly red. But if the light passes through larger particles, such as water droplets, you tend to get paler light. A ruddy sky at sunset, then, can indicate that there is little moisture in the upper atmosphere west of you, where tomorrow's weather generally comes from—and thus sunny skies are in the forecast. It might also be a situation, say some meteorologists, in which the setting sun is simply reflecting off the underside of clouds on the eastern horizon, which suggests that rainy weather has already moved beyond you.

The second part of the proverb is the subject of endless speculation among professional meteorologists. More importantly, it isn't the least bit reliable. So when morning comes, sailor, don't even bother looking for red in the sky: you'd do just as well to flip a coin.

Q What is that smell when it rains?
—*Chris St. John, Fort Myers, Florida*

A It's not rain you're smelling; it's dirt. The piquant, musky odor that hangs in the air emanates from an odorous chemical buried in the soil called *geosmin* (literally, "earth smell"). One way to detect that "rain" scent is to unearth the geosmin yourself by rooting around in your garden. But a good rain shower will do the trick as well. As a storm moves in, the atmospheric pressure drops and equalizes with the pressure in the ground, causing the earth to "outgas" geosmin. "When the barometric pressure drops, the soil exhales," explains Mary Firestone, a soil microbiologist at the University of California, Berkeley. Because odors transmit more efficiently in wet air, a mere hint of geosmin is enough to get our olfactories primed for a shower.

Q What do tornadoes have against trailer parks?

—Crowley Tucker, Fayetteville, Arkansas

A There's a lot of conventional wisdom about where tornadoes will and will not go, and virtually all of it is false. You'll hear that they do not cross rivers. You'll hear that they avoid cities and refuse to climb hills. The reality? Twisters have crossed the Mississippi and the Ohio, to name just two rivers. They've struck in Denver, St. Louis, Lubbock, Topeka, and Kalamazoo, among other cities. One resolute funnel in 1989 climbed the continental divide into Grand Teton National Park, devastating a forest along a sixty-mile path. It's hard to predict where they'll go.

As for trailer parks: Although it's tempting to think of God as an architectural snob keen on ridding the countryside of unsightly fiberglass, when you look into it you find that the trailer park–tornado connection is only a misconstrued impression. Studies show that tornadoes, aimless wanderers that they are, don't hit trailer parks any more than they hit anything else. It's just that when they do, the death toll is nearly always high, because mobile homes are so dangerously . . . mobile. In 1994, 40 percent of all

Americans killed by tornadoes lived in trailers, though trailers accounted for only 6 percent of U.S. housing. Homes with good sturdy foundations stand at least a fighting chance of enduring a twister—all the more reason to build your existence on solid ground.

Q Do frogs really rain from the skies?

—Georgia Spencer, Newport, Rhode Island

A Ignore all harumphing fuddy-duddies who say that this phenomenon is preposterous: It happens, and with greater frequency than you'd guess. The skies are constantly dropping stuff, and not just frogs. There are well-documented stories of crabs, birds, spiders, turtles, snails, crayfish, maggots, and even livestock raining down from the firmament. In 1997 a Korean fisherman was knocked unconscious by a frozen lump of heaven-sent squid. And a Japanese vessel sank in 1990 after being clobbered by a falling cow. How does this happen? In most cases, the culprit is a waterspout or tornado that has sucked up the unsuspecting wildlife into the upper registers of a powerful storm cell—often freezing them before hurling them earthward with the rain, sometimes up to twenty miles away from where they started. Although nature obviously isn't picky about its victims, young froglets and tadpoles do seem to be especially good candidates for this sort of mass animal hoovering. They're just the right size—small, but offering enough wind resistance and heft to get airborne. And they can be outrageously prolific. Considering that a single frog can lay as many as twenty thousand eggs, a funnel that happens to make a direct hit along the banks of a lake or pond a few weeks after all those eggs have hatched can vacuum up untold legions of amphibians and blow them sky-high. You'll be glad to know that they don't all perish, however. In 1954, thousands of live juvenile frogs "came down like snowflakes" on the West Midlands of Great Britain, over an area of fifty square yards. And in 1882, eyewitnesses in Dubuque, Iowa, reported finding a hailstone that contained two frogs in it. The frogs crawled away after the ice melted—alive and well, if a little dazed from their ordeal.

Q Where does smog go after it rains? Does it harm anything?

—Ingrid Stephens, Mesa, Arizona

A Every year urban dwellers brace for the Brown Season, those summer and early fall months in which hot air masses squat on layers of cool air, trapping all the ick of city life in a low-lying holding pattern. Combine this dreaded temperature inversion with hot, ozone-producing sunlight and mountains to check the breeze, and you get what meteorologists refer to as a *smog episode*. In short, you get Los Angeles, or Mexico City, or Phoenix. When this happens, the sweetest relief is rain. A storm comes along and presto, all that acrid stuff is magically gone. But gone where? Some of it, especially particulate matter, gets "ingested" into water droplets and washes down on you in the form of acid rain, whose harmful effects we're all too familiar with. Some of it goes skyward, pushed into the upper atmosphere by the storm's turbulence, where it can haunt you with an encore performance a few days later. The rest is blown free and clear of your fine, spewing metropolis and then ultimately becomes someone else's problem (for example, researchers have long been trying to determine whether L.A. smog contributes to troubling bouts of hazy visibility at the Grand Canyon). Miraculous though they might seem, rainstorms don't wash away smog; they just spread it around.

did i just see that?

Q Recently, I spotted what appeared to be three suns in the western sky. What was that about?

—Deb McCorvey, Littleton, Colorado

A Most likely, you were the lucky witness to *sun dogs*. Also known as *parhelia* or *mock suns*, they are the result of a dazzling optical effect (thought to be the likeliest explanation behind many UFO sightings) that can be seen year-round but are more likely to occur during winter months. In the hour or so after sunrise or before sunset, when the sun is low in the sky, the angled rays can refract through hexagonal ice crystals in high, cold cirrus clouds, causing a shimmery, orange-rimmed duplicate on one or both sides of the fiery orb. "You're seeing images of the sun that have been displaced twenty-two degrees," explains Margaret LeMone of the National Center for Atmospheric Research, who goes on to offer a savvy explanation of the canine sobriquet. "They seem to follow the sun around like a dog." Legend has it that the Mandan Indians of North Dakota interpreted this dazzling triptych in a more practical way: it's so cold on the Great Plains that the sun lights little fires on each side of it to stay warm.

Q My girlfriend claims she once saw a "lightning ball" on a camping trip. Should she get her eyes examined? Or her head?

—Ian Maloney, San Francisco, California

A The phenomenon of *ball lightning*—small glowing spheres observed during thunderstorms and even in placid weather—has long been written off as either an optical illusion or superstition. But in the last decade, thousands of eyewitness accounts have been studied in Russia and Japan, and now most scientists are believers.

Which isn't to say they understand it. Ball lightning is weird stuff. The name is a misnomer because it doesn't really behave much like lightning. It's been known to drop down chimneys, pass through windows, and form suddenly in rooms. In one memorable case, a lightning ball floated down an airplane aisle. Sometimes it's cool to the touch; other times it's hot enough to boil water or melt glass. It usually lasts about five seconds, after which it can vanish quietly or explode.

Ball lightning has been invoked to explain everything from spontaneous human combustion to the odd atmospheric lights of Marfa, Texas. But what is it? The leading theory is that it's *plasma*—atmospheric gas ionized by conventional lightning. Indeed, two Japanese physicists have used microwaves to create tiny plasma balls in the laboratory. Whatever it is, fewer than one person in a thousand will encounter ball lightning over the course of a lifetime. So hang on to your girlfriend: she's a rare find.

Q I've heard there are certain prevailing conditions that create huge mirages in the Arctic. Is there anything to this?
—*Tamara Morris, Great Falls, Virginia*

A This is the fabled *Fata Morgana,* an optical illusion that has been known to propagate whole cities, armadas, and mountain ranges where none exist. The phenomenon generally occurs over vast expanses of ice or water where distances are difficult to judge, and for reasons that aren't entirely clear, it seems to be especially common in the Arctic and in the Straits of Messina separating Italy from Sicily. The precise optics are not entirely understood, but, simply put, Fata Morganas are created when the light bouncing off faraway objects is refracted through the atmospheric "lens" created by different thermal layers, a process that, when conditions are just right, can dramatically distort and magnify the original image; sometimes the same image can be repeated and, in effect, piled upon itself several times, so that an iceberg looks like a skyscraper or a hill assumes Himalayan proportions. *Fata Morgana* is Italian for "the fairy Morgan," the sorceress of Arthurian legend who was said to have a talent for bending shapes and lofting castles in the sky. Atmospheric scientists believe Fata Morganas might explain such phantasms as the legend of the Flying Dutchman. But perhaps the most infamous example of a Fata Morgana was "Crockerland," the nonexistent Arctic country that Robert Peary, a man with an Active imagination to start with, reported seeing on a 1906 expedition to the far reaches of North America. "It was with a thrill that my glasses revealed the white summits of a distant land," he wrote at the time. Seven years later, the Museum of Natural History dispatched a costly expedition to explore Crockerland, and found nothing but the same tantalizing mirage.

Q Caribbean sunsets often are said to climax with something called "the green flash." Is it real, or just a margarita side effect?

—Frank King, Nashua, New Hampshire

A No, the green flash really happens. It's a bit tricky to explain all the science in layman's terms, but it has to do with the way the atmosphere works like a prism, bending the last rays of the sinking sun and selectively scattering the blue end of the spectrum. If conditions are right, just before the final sliver of sun vanishes, and just for a second, it'll turn a vivid emerald hue. Actually, the green flash is visible at both sunset and sunrise, and not just in the Tropics. But it tends to be most visible over the sea or other places where the horizon is especially low, and on nights that are perfectly clear. There are spots where it's commonplace—Hawaii, for instance—though no one seems to know exactly why.

Q Double rainbows are fairly common. But has anyone ever seen a triple rainbow?

—Bill Menzies, El Paso, Texas

A There are credible reports of all kinds of permutations on the rainbow theme: Fogbows. Sandbows. Infrared rainbows. But there's never been a verified sighting of a true triple rainbow. As you might know, a rainbow appears when the sun is behind you, shining on a

Did I just see that?

147

patch of rain or mist that's in front of you. Says Wisconsin physicist and rainbow ace Robert Greenler, "The primary rainbow is created when light rays shine into the droplets, reflect once, and come out. Rays that reflect twice create the secondary rainbow." But what about rays that reflect three times? They ought to create a third rainbow, right? Theoretically. But the question is, where do you look for it? "The assumption was that it must be near the primary and secondary rainbows, only fainter," says Greenler. "Yet when you do the physics, it turns out the tertiary rainbow would be on the other side of the sky, seen as a circle around the sun."

In 1914 the *Journal of the Royal Meteorological Society* reported an incident in which parts of six bows were observed simultaneously. This sighting did not count as an official sextuple, however; most likely it was just a double rainbow accompanied by *supernumeraries,* little fragments of the primary rainbow that crop up under certain conditions. So if you see what appears to be a triple or triple-plus rainbow, it's probably not the real McCoy.

Q A friend insists that the aurora borealis makes a noise. Am I going deaf?

—*Dave Malinowski, State College, Pennsylvania*

A For a long time people have been "hearing" the northern lights—a low crackling or hissing—and today most experts believe it's real. It usually occurs on cold, still nights when the aurora is especially active. Strangely, the noise seems to come from the ground, not the sky. Probably what people are hearing isn't the aurora itself—which after all is some sixty miles up—but vibrations that the aurora produces in snow or pine needles. The signal might even bypass the ears and work directly on the brain, creating the sensation of sound. Like the so-called Taos Hum of New Mexico, some people hear it and others don't. "After thirty-one years in Alaska, I've never heard it," notes Neal Brown of the Geophysical Institute in Fairbanks. "But it's been heard by people I was standing next to." Even if you can't hear the aurora, you can at least capture its low-frequency radio emanations: rig yourself a twenty-foot-long wire antenna, plug it into the microphone jack of your tape player, and hit *record*.

moonstruck

Q Does the full moon really get animals riled up, or is that an old wives' tale?

—*Agatha Robinson, South Bend, Indiana*

A As is implied by the very word *lunatic*, it has long been held that the full moon makes animals, including humans, go crazy. Even today, you will be anecdoted to death about the moon's mysterious biochemical power over our moods and life processes. You'll hear about something that's been called *the biological tides*, the notion that because our bodies are 80 percent water, we must be profoundly affected by the moon's gravitational pull just as the oceans are. You'll also hear that more births occur around the full moon and that the murder rate rises precipitously.

Is there anything to any of this? Well, yes and no—but mostly no. Even though it's more than 250,000 miles away from us, our only natural satellite does exert a certain influence on the mating patterns of animals—especially marine animals, which should not be too surprising, as the moon also governs the tides. The reproductive cycles of sea urchins, fiddler crabs, oysters, and the California grunion, to cite just a few examples, are intimately tied to the lunar calendar. Dive the Great Barrier Reef on the evening of the full moon, and you'll be treated to the amazing spectacle of thousands of coral polyps simultaneously releasing clouds of sperm and eggs in a kind of psychedelic mass orgy timed to coincide with the month's highest tide. Then too, many species of terrestrial wildlife seem to be more active on the night of a full moon, but most likely they're simply responding to the fact that a full-moon evening stays brighter, and brighter longer, than other nights, thus affording better vision for mating, hunting, and foraging.

There is no solid evidence, however, that the full moon makes any of us in the animal kingdom discernibly more agitated or deranged than we already are. The few studies of scientific rigor that *have* been done indicate that all these "moonstruck" theories are pure rubbish. In one such analysis completed in 1985, Nicholas Sanduleak, a Case Western Reserve University astronomer, reviewed statistics on 3,370 Cleveland homicides over an eleven-year span and found no correlation whatsoever with the moon's waxing and waning. Reviewing several similar national studies, Sanduleak found that "no conclusive statistical evidence exists for the reality of any kind of lunar effect on human behavior." Most scientists believe that to the extent that the moon has any measurable effect on our moods and behaviors, it's purely psychological.

Q Is it possible to see a rainbow at night?

—Van Taylor, Orlando, Florida

A No, not exactly. But there is a little-known phenomenon known as a *moonbow*, a ghostly white arc that appears when the light of a full or almost full moon is refracted in a waterfall's mist. But whereas rainbows require only a smattering of raindrops and a few rays of sun, moonbows are decidedly more finicky: the falls must be in front of you and the moon at forty-two degrees in the sky behind you; the water must produce a heavy mist; and the river gorge must be wide enough to let in plenty of moonlight. This helps explain why Kentucky's Cumberland Falls and southern Africa's Victoria Falls are the only places known to yield moonbows on a regular basis. Niagara Falls used to have one until air pollution and city lights obscured it. All that's left now is an artificial "neonbow," compliments of the reflections of nearby No Vacancy signs.

Q What causes the "man in the moon" effect?

—Rebecca Roth, Calgary, Alberta, Canada

A Most astronomers pooh-pooh the existence of the man in the moon. "I've never seen it," says Frank Summers of New York's Hayden Planetarium, "and I don't know anyone who has." All the same, people have reported seeing things in the moon for millennia. The Egyptians thought the moon was a dog-headed ape, whereas in ancient China the moon was widely viewed as a hare. In the nineteenth century, the man in the moon shared equal billing with the crab in the moon, the lady in the moon, the girl reading in the moon, and the donkey in the moon. We see what we want to see up there, it seems, but our imagination is aided by the moon's multicolored topography, particularly the contrast between its gray, powdery soils and the swaths of dark lava that form the *lunar seas*. It's these basalt seas that are said to form the man's "eyes" and "mouth." But don't tell that to learned astronomers. "The man in the moon is just an expression," says Noreen Grice of Boston's Museum of Science. "No, it's an illusion. No, I know: It's a perception. *That's* what it is."

Q What's a blue moon? Does it really look blue?

—Bob Busch, Kansas City, Missouri

A *Blue moon* refers to the second full moon in a calendar month, which happens about every 2.73 years.

No one is really sure why it's called that. Certainly it has nothing to do with color. A blue moon looks no different from any other full moon. In medieval times, people used the expression *blue moon* to connote an absurd situation, but nowadays it signifies any event that's infrequent but unpinpointable.

A wrinkle: Sometimes the moon really does appear blue. Any natural disaster that sends large amounts of particulate matter into the atmosphere—a forest fire, say—can scatter light at the red end of the spectrum, causing the moon to take on a bruiselike tint. Perhaps the most prolonged example of this occurred in 1883, when Indonesia's Krakatoa volcano spewed ash around the world. The moon appeared blue for months.

What did astronomers call the second full moon of the month before *blue moon* became common? "Nothing," says John Mosley of the Griffith Observatory. "What do you call the second Tuesday of the month? There's no need to name it."

Q What makes the world turn—is it the gravitational tug of the moon?

—Eric Craig, Louisville, Kentucky

A Our planet doesn't rotate because of something that's happening now. Something set it going aeons ago, and though it's gradually slowing down, it's got many more aeons to go before it stops. What kind of something?

Here's the leading theory: The solar system formed out of dust and gas left over from the making of the sun. Little chunks of matter gradually gathered into bigger chunks, as gravity worked its magic. Eventually, about 4.5 billion years ago, a very large chunk—the size of Mars—is thought to have collided with Earth. "It was really a titanic collision," says Luke Dones of NASA's Ames Research Center. "It hit off-center, so it set Earth spinning." (Some of the debris from this collision, incidentally, is believed to have been thrown into orbit, forming our moon.)

Earth really got to twirling after that collision; a day might have been as short as four hours. Since then the pace has slowed considerably because of a process known as *tidal friction*. The tides, of course, occur when the Moon's gravity raises a bulge in the ocean. To oversimplify a bit, the Moon tries to hold on to the bulge while Earth's rotation tries to move it away, with the net effect that Earth turns a little slower (and the Moon revolves around it a little faster) with each rotation. The slowdown isn't what you'd call drastic—only a few thousandths of a second per century—but forewarned is forearmed: Eventually there's going to be a day that lasts forever. What do you want to bet it's a Monday?

billions and billions

Q I've heard that space is teeming with death rays capable of destroying all life on Earth. Please tell me this isn't true.

—*Angus McMahon, Frankfurt, Kentucky*

A In the early morning hours on January 28, 1999, astronomers in Los Alamos, New Mexico, captured something astonishingly powerful on film: Lasting only about ten seconds, it was by far the brightest and most violent explosion ever detected in the history of science, a cosmic detonation second only to the Big Bang itself. Astronomers call these distant explosions *gamma ray bursts* (GRBs). They're one of the truly frightening enigmas of the heavens, something out of Arthur C. Clarke. First discovered back in 1967, GRBs are now detected at a rate of about one or two per day. They're believed to be a kind of last gasp of radiation released in the final seconds before dying "neutron" stars collapse into black holes. Though it was unprecedentedly bright, the January 28 burst posed no dangers to our planet because it originated some nine billion light-years away, so far back in space-time as to be inconsequential to us. But what would happen if one of these cataclysmic events occurred here in our own galaxy? "It would quite simply be the worst natural disaster you could ever imagine," says NASA astrophysicist Peter Leonard of the Compton Gamma Ray Observatory. "The ozone layer would be destroyed, much of the planet would be cooked in a cosmic ray bath, and Earth would stay radioactive for millions of years." In other words, our planet would be largely sterilized, the biological slate swept clean. How likely is this doomsday scenario (an event Leonard likes to call a "burst in the hood")? Well, actually, it's probably already happened. There is good evidence that these radioactive explosions have gone off in our galaxy before—maverick scientists, in fact, have lately begun to speculate that past gamma ray bursts might explain some of the mass extinctions in Earth's geological record. And certainly there's no reason to believe we'll be spared these intragalactic pyrotechnics in the future. Astronomers believe that the Milky Way might experience a gamma ray burst every two hundred million years or so, and there are plenty of moribund stars in our galaxy that could make likely candidates for the next

Armageddon. (Happily for us, most projections estimate that the next detonation is probably still millions of years off). For better or worse, there's probably nothing we—or rather, our descendants—can do to stop the death rays, or even see them coming. Says Leonard: "It's difficult to make out the gun, when you're staring down its barrel."

Q I hear Tom Cruise has a star named after him. How do I get mine?

—Amanda Dawson, Bozeman, Montana

A Mr. Cruise's star is called Forever Tom, and it resides in the constellation Hercules. You can see it by pointing your telescope at R.A. $16^h55^m45^s$, ∂ 47°39'. The name was duly purchased by Cruise's then wife, Nicole Kidman, from the International Star Registry, the world's largest such outfit, with nearly five hundred thousand points of light claimed to date. For $45, you can christen your own star ("Our inventory is limitless," the company claims), and you'll receive a handsome astral deed. But the name will have no currency among astronomers. No one will ever say, "Captain, we have detected enemy vessels approaching from the Amanda Dawson supernova." And there is always the risk that someone will go to a competing registry and claim your star for himself. The fact is, the International Astronomers Union (IAU) in Paris doesn't bother naming stars—it merely numbers them. Yet this needn't dash your hopes for cosmic immortality. If you can get in the good graces of an astronomer who's on the brink of a discovery, it's still possible to get your name on, say, an asteroid or a lunar crater. You must exercise restraint, however: in 1985, astronomer James Gibson created such a stir by designating an asteroid Mr. Spock, after his cat, that the IAU passed a resolution "discouraging" the naming of celestial bodies after pets.

Q What exactly was the Star of Bethlehem, and can I still see it today?

—Oliver Hays, New York, New York

A This question has long bothered faithful skywatchers unwilling to dismiss the Bible's most famous star as simply a bit of scriptural license or a genuine heaven-sent miracle thus requiring no scientific explanation. Drawing from ancient astronomical records, theorists have speculated that the celestial beacon that drew the Magi to Bethlehem might in fact have been a supernova, Halley's Comet, or even Venus. The most promising hypothesis to date, however, is that the mysterious star was merely an optical illusion formed by the *conjunction*, or close approach, of Jupiter and Saturn. This occurs every nine hundred years or so, making it appear as though the two planets have merged into a single luminescent body. Conveniently, one such conjunction is thought to have happened right around the time of the historical Jesus' birth, somewhere between 7 and 5 B.C. Inconveniently, however, computer models show that this long-ago celestial pairing occurred sometime in August or September, which means Christmas should actually be a summer holiday.

Q In a novel I was reading recently, the writer mentions something called a "false dawn." Is that a real thing or just a precious writerly expression?

—Simon Hutchinson, Savannah, Georgia

A No, it's real. The false dawn is one of the great understated spectacles of the solar system. *Zodiacal light,* or *false dawn* as it's known colloquially, is a pale-yellow glow that appears in the eastern sky two hours before sunrise. The cause: tiny silicate debris that has been ejected from comets or left over from the creation of the solar system—a kind of cosmic talc that orbits our sun in an enormous elliptical disc. The rising sun's light bounces off these grains of space dust, creating a spectral glow in the shape of a cone. To us, it looks as if there's a bright metropolis just over the next hill. But false dawn is a rare and fragile thing, and when it happens, it doesn't last long. To glimpse it, you've usually got to situate yourself in an extremely dark part of the world, with crisp night skies untainted by city lights. It's visible only when the sun's rays are in perfect alignment with the orbiting crumbs and when the predawn sky is moonless and black (the faintest twilight of true dawn is enough to kill the effect). In North America, false dawns peak in October.

Q Is Pluto really a planet?

—Jack Durant, Essex, Maryland

A After assiduous campaigning by its discoverers at Arizona's Lowell Observatory, distant Pluto was hastily declared a planet in 1930, and ever since then schoolchildren have been taught with great conviction that there are nine large bodies, or "major planets," revolving around our Sun. Yet if it were discovered today, Pluto would certainly not make the grade in the majors. For starters, it's too small—less than half the size of Mercury and smaller than our own Moon—and it has no gravitational influence on the orbits of the other eight planets. Brutal as it might seem, Pluto has been demoted, though since the early nineties scientists have been haggling over what diminutive name it deserves: asteroid, minor body, dwarf planet, or perhaps the ultimate slap, *planetesimal.* Whatever Pluto is, it's one of the true oddities of our solar system, a ball of frozen methane that has an elliptical orbit and behaves rather like a comet. "It's a fascinating minor body," concedes astronomer Daniel Green of the Harvard-Smithsonian Center for Astrophysics. "But no one seriously calls Pluto a major planet anymore, except for a couple of whiners who're stuck in the 1930s."

Q What makes stars twinkle?

—Michael Miller, Wheat Ridge, Colorado

A You know that when you dip a stick in the water, it looks strangely bent. That's *refraction,* the tendency of light to change direction when it moves from one medium (such as air) to another (such as water). The same principle makes stars do the magical thing they do. As light travels from the star toward your eye, it passes through the turbulent upper atmosphere. Up there, rivers of air flow in all directions, constantly changing in temperature and density and therefore refracting light differently. Starlight gets jiggled through all this chaos. Your eye registers the motion as twinkling. At the same time, interference patterns make the light grow rapidly brighter and darker, and the changes of refraction that cause twinkling also cause a steady stream of variations in the star's color. If there were no atmosphere, the stars would burn bright and steady: pretty, but not especially poetic. You can think of twinkling as a kind of signal degradation, but hey, *vive l'interference.*

But why, you might ask, don't *planets* twinkle? Stars are so far away that to us they're mere point sources of light; that is, there's just one path for the light to follow from, say, Alpha Centauri to your eye, so the slightest distortion will make it appear to twinkle. Not so the visible planets, which, even though they send us only reflected light, are much closer and occupy more space in the sky. Light from East Venus will follow a slightly different path to your eyeball than light from West Venus. There might be some twinkle on each separate path, but when you put them all together, your eye averages things out and you get a nice sober glow.

Q How far does space go? It can't just stop like a wall.

—Tommy Estes, Tupelo, Mississippi

A Like all great stoner questions, this one is infinitely large and infinitely deep—and its answer is fundamentally unsatisfying. We do know this: Hubble Telescope findings portray an enormous universe that stretches some thirty billion light-years across. Scientists agree that it's been expanding outward in all directions ever since the big bang, twelve to fifteen billion years ago. But what is it expanding *into?* Sadly, we don't know, and we'll never be able to outrace the expansion to find out. "If we could freeze time and travel to the distant reaches of the universe, then we might be able to learn what, if anything, is out there beyond it," says Hubble senior project scientist David Leckrone. "Obviously that will never happen." To get in the proper frame of mind for contemplating this question, you've got to stop conceptualizing space in conventional ways and step into the worldview of Salvador Dalí, with his melting clocks and can't-get-there-from-here perspectives. "You can't think of the universe as one thing expanding inside another thing, like a balloon in a room," says Leckrone. "The universe is a closed geometry. The expanding balloon is all there is." Leckrone suggests what is perhaps a better analogy, although it, too, falls short: We (that is those of us here in the known universe) are like ants crawling around on the inside surface of a sealed glass jar. We'll never find an outside. If there is anything beyond the glass, we just don't have the ability to observe, measure, or even fathom it. In other words, science demurs, and the fuzzier realms of metaphysics and theology take over.

Unsatisfied? So are we.

Q Why are planets basically round? You'd think they'd be more irregularly shaped, much like meteors.
—Holly Childs, Gastonia, South Carolina

A Imagine you're building a stone tower, miles into the sky. At some point, you'll come up against the fundamental limitations of the materials you're working with: Your Tower of Babel will crumble from its own weight, the ground will sag beneath it—it simply won't get any taller. Something similar happens with celestial bodies. In effect, once a clod of space rock gets up to a certain size, its gravity causes it to cave in on itself, smoothing out the biggest bumps, pocks, and other surface irregularities. Smaller rocks, like asteroids and meteors, don't have the same gravitational forces to contend with. "A celestial rock that's only two hundred miles across can be quite irregular," notes David Morrison of NASA's Ames Research Center. "But you'll find that once asteroids get up to, say, seven hundred miles across, they're usually pretty spherical." If Earth were made entirely of gases and liquids, it would not only assume a spherical shape but gravity would pull everything down to a perfectly smooth, even surface. But solid rock, to varying degrees, can withstand gravity's pull—which explains why, despite its overall orblike appearance, Earth tolerates mountains, valleys, hills, and other idiosyncrasies.

Q Do the planets really make a faint "music" that you can hear?

—Rita Sousalous, Davenport, Iowa

A It's a beautiful idea, this ancient notion of the "music of the spheres," but like so many beautiful ideas, it's hopelessly wrong. The Pythagorean mathematicians of ancient Greece are said to have been the ones who originated the theory that the planets and stars whirl about us with such elegance and perfect proportionality that they actually play an ethereal harmony that can be heard by the naked ear, if the stargazer is willing to listen intently enough (and drink enough wine). Of course this is entirely imaginary, the kind of rapturous sentiment that only a mathematics-crazed mystic could have dreamed up. The Pythagoreans argued that the cosmos was pleasingly purposeful, like a lyre strung up for our benefit, and we lucky earthlings were sitting in the sweet spot at the center of the whole celestial show. Even after Copernicus figured out that, on the contrary, the sun was at the hub of things, the idea of the music of the spheres wouldn't go away. "Give air to the heaven," wrote German astronomer Johannes Kepler in the late 1590s, "and truly and really there will be music . . . which pure spirits sense with no less enjoyment than man experiences when listening to musical chords." In his *Harmonice Mundi* of 1619, Kepler went on to assign actual notes and harmonic relationships to the different planets, and this, in turn, inspired classical musicians from Johann Strauss to Gustav Holst to attempt their own interpretations of the celestial spheres. Today, of course, we know that far from being serene, outer space is a place of volatility and crashing violence—dying stars, smashing asteroids, greedy black holes. We can't exactly hear any of this ruckus, since sound doesn't travel in the vacuum of space. The best astronomers can do is train their radio telescopes on the heavens, and when they do, they pick up a deafening cacophony of clicks and bumps and fizzes. It's a discordant world out there, more Johnny Rotten than Johann Strauss.

further life forms

scales and tails

Dispatches from reptilia, amphibia

Q Why are lizards always doing push-ups?

—Jim Caldwell, Torrance, California

A It's a form of communication. Lizards use the *push-up display*, as it's called, to announce their presence to the world, to attract mates, and to warn competitors off their turf—basically to say "Yo!" "Yo, baby!" or "Yo' mama!" The precise message depends on the number of push-ups, the position of the tail and legs, and whether the lizard puffs up his throat. ("His" throat because males appear to do push-ups with greater frequency than females.) According to University of Oregon biology professor Emilia Martins, whose dissertation involved 150 hours in the field watching some 1,600 calisthenic incidents performed by sagebrush lizards (seriously!), a push-up that means one thing when no one's around can acquire a different significance when, say, an eligible female is sunning herself on the next rock. It's a shame people never picked up on this form of language. Not only would we be more dynamic conversationalists, but, like Jack LaLanne, we'd all be in terrific shape.

Q So what *is* the difference between a frog and a toad?

—Alison Bart, Lynchburg, Virginia

A Some "authorities," such as Webelo troop masters and various witches stirring bubbling cauldrons, will swear up and down that there's an absolute, clear-cut distinction between these two groups of amphibians, but they're mistaken. From the standpoint of anatomy, metabolism, and evolutionary lineage, frogs and toads are basically one and the same; serious herpetologists make no formal distinction. To them, they're all frogs, members of the multitudinous order *Anura*. The word *toad* is a bit of sloppy—albeit handy—slang that we have long used to describe those homely members of the family *Bufonidae*, creatures that tend to have drier, wartier skin, a squatter physique, less pronounced foot-webbing, and a preference for dry land. But even these general differences come with notable exceptions. For example, there are highly aquatic "toads"

(like the Suriname toad), and there are any number of frogs (such as the barking tree frog) that avoid water altogether except to breed. There are warty frogs with dry hides, and slimy toads with webbed feet. To compound the imprecision, sometimes a given species of amphibian might be known as a frog in one locality, and a toad three counties over. Not only are toads not toads, technically speaking, some of them aren't even frogs—such as the horny toad, which is actually a lizard. For all of these reasons, insists San Diego herpetological authority Chuck Crumley of the San Diego Natural History Museum, "the whole frog/toad dichotomy is without scientific validity. It's artificial, it's slangy, and it's imprecise!" By God, let's put a stop to it.

Q How do chameleons change their colors?

—Terry Latham, Joplin, Missouri

A Chalk it up to a bad case of the jitters. The chameleon's nervous system activates special skin cells called *chromatophores,* which contain pigments capable of moving either toward or away from the surface of the skin. The pigments that migrate closest to the surface determine its current color. Interestingly, only a handful of the 150-odd species of chameleons can deliberately blend in with their background. The rest change color for more mundane reasons: to impress a mate, warm themselves by donning a darker shade, or scare off predators by deploying bright, kaleidoscopic bursts of color. This last strategy might sound counterintuitive (wouldn't startling splashes of color serve more as advertisement than deterrent to a potential diner?), but as California chameleon breeder Linda Davison points out, "When you're a tiny jungle snack living among 12-foot-long mamba snakes, you've got to be creative."

Q How is it that a community of frogs can appear seemingly overnight, inhabiting a small puddle that only exists a few weeks a year?

—Jeff Morgan, Kansas City, Missouri

A This is not a case of spontaneous frog generation, although it might appear so; these mystery amphibians usually come from underground burrows and crevasses, where they can lie in a kind of zombie-like state for months or even years, waiting for the right gully washer to create just such a puddle. It might seem like a tenuous way to live, but in many precincts of the world, especially in arid climes, there are numerous species of frogs (such as the Mexican burrower or the water-holding frog of the Australian Outback) that build their existence around the sudden appearance of what the experts refer to as *ephemeral pools*. A good summer storm sails through and—shazam!—that very night the slumbering frogs awaken to the moisture and lurch from their underground crypts, with only sex on their mind. "They're what we call explosive breeders," notes University of Missouri frog specialist Ray Semlitsch. "Most of the time they're invisible and then suddenly they appear after a rainstorm, as if by magic, to lay eggs." For these time-starved amphibians, it's a desperate frenzy designed to make maximum use of an extremely narrow window of procreative opportunity. The tadpoles might hatch within a single day, and if all goes well, they'll metamorphose into tiny froglets in two to three weeks. Regrettably, the majority doesn't outlive the race against evaporation. All across the land you can find the killing ponds: scummed-over watering holes strewn with the corpses of shriveled tadpoles. Those that do make it (many of them having resorted to Donner-party cannibalism to survive their fast-shrinking universe) will hop out of their puddles and corkscrew themselves back into their sandy burrows, where they lower their metabolic rate and secrete a sticky goo to help preserve themselves until the next trysting lagoon is born.

Q Do crocodiles really cry?
—Milton James, Los Angeles, California

A The image of the crocodile manufacturing tears before dining on its prey has been a handy metaphor for insincerity since medieval times. "If the crocodile findeth a man by the brim of the water," wrote Bartholomaeus Anglicus in his 1250 encyclopedia *De proprietatibus rerum,* "he weepeth upon him, and swalloweth him at last."

Is there anything to it? Yes and no. Crocodiles do apparently have lachrymal glands. Frank Mazzotti, a University of Florida wildlife scientist who's worked with crocs for seventeen years, has spotted what appear to be excreted droplets around their eyes. Other saltwater reptiles, such as sea turtles, are known to "cry" as a way of purging sodium, and Mazzotti believes something similar might be going on with crocodiles. But you can't truly say this ancient reptile "weepeth," for according to experts it has no capacity for emotion, feigned or otherwise. (Herpetologist Ken Vliet once compared its mental state to "a dial tone.") So all that insincerity business is just a croc.

Q How do you extract the poison from a poison-dart frog?

—Lynn Spalding, Johnson City, Tennessee

A In western Colombia, where the blowgun is still part of the hunter's kit, they do it by roasting one of two frog species (*Phyllobates aurotaenia* or *Phyllobates bicolor*) on a spit and collecting the toxic liquid exuded by the skin. Researchers there recently learned of another species, *Phyllobates terribilis*, which is so poisonous that natives only have to scrape a dart across its back. "I wouldn't touch that frog," notes John Daly, who studies frog juice for the National Institutes of Health. "It has enough toxin to kill lots of people, far more than it needs." If you're hatching some fiendish scheme, Lynn, bear this in mind: Of the seventy known species of poison-dart frogs, only the aforementioned three are poisonous enough to merit a place in the aboriginal arsenal. But because these frogs derive their poison from their forest diet, their toxicity fades once they leave the wild. So the pet-shop versions are duds.

Q I've heard that baby snakes are more poisonous than adults. Is this possible?

—Marcus Horn, Steamboat Springs, Colorado

A Like Athena, a venomous snake springs from its mother's egg fully formed and ready for business—in this case, with an ample supply of toxins that, yes, are often more poisonous than those of their parents. Reptile experts haven't proved conclusively why this is so, but they do offer up several hypotheses. One theory is that because newborns haven't used their venom yet, and thus haven't been forced to regenerate it, the poison is more potent. Another suggests that infant venom contains a higher percentage of water, which might speed its absorption into the victim's blood. There is a bit of good news, however. Though the toxicity can be greater, the yield is always smaller, as tiny snake babies have proportionately tiny venom sacs. What's more, they're not very skilled at hurling themselves at prey or projecting their poison. Still, should a western diamondback not much bigger than a night crawler sink its miniature fangs into you, you're in for a very bad time. "You can expect necrosis of the tissue to set in," says Bill Haast, a venomologist at the Miami Serpentarium. "Your flesh will dissolve, your skin will slough off, and there may be permanent scarring." And that's not to mention the pain. "I can't describe the agony," recalls Christie Kroll, a Putnam Valley, New York, animal-rescue specialist who a few years ago was struck on her thumb by a baby copperhead that was only three inches long. "I didn't pay attention to it at first, but then the venom burned a hole down to the bone, and ended up costing me $15,000 in medical and plastic surgery bills."

Q Where do frogs spend their winters?

—Amy Wilkes, San Diego, California

A What's the matter—have you never seen those little green V-formations hopping south? Actually, frogs and toads hibernate. Some winter at the bottom of ponds and lakes. Others dig below the frost line. And still others crawl under logs or leaf litter. These last guys are interesting, as they're often exposed to subfreezing temperatures. At least five frog species, including the wood frog and the spring peeper, can cope with temperatures as low as eighteen degrees Fahrenheit. Their hearts stop and their fluids turn to ice; when the weather warms up, they recover.

So how do they do it? As the mercury drops, they produce large amounts of glucose, which counteracts the cell

shrinkage that occurs during freezing. They also elimi-
nate fluid from their organs. Miami University biologist
Jon Costanzo says the liver of a freezing frog loses 50
percent of its moisture and "has the consistency of beef
jerky."

insectascience

All creatures creep and crawl

Q Why are moths drawn to light and what do they get out of it?
—Emily Allen, Waco, Texas

A The moth, specifically the male moth, is attracted to an illuminated lightbulb for the sad but simple reason that it thinks it's the moon. For roughly 150 million years, the visually impaired lepidopterans relied on the giant orb to help them navigate in a straight line, always keeping the moon's rays at a constant angle during their nightly mating excursions—flying a more or less steady course until they caught the scent of a female perched on a nearby leaf. But moth history took an unfortunate twist when the incandescent lamp arrived on the scene in 1879.

"Moths will never forgive Thomas Edison," says Cornell University entomologist Cole Gilbert, noting that chaos ensued as the nocturnal creatures began mistaking light-bulbs for the moon. Unfortunately, flying so close to these surrogate moons makes it nearly impossible for a moth to maintain a straight course, so it must constantly correct its bearing. Soon it becomes completely confused and disoriented. "Before you know it," says Gilbert, "the poor guy is fluttering around in circles." Relief comes only when the moth resigns itself to a celibate night on a strange porch, waiting until dawn, when it can find its way back into the thickets to fly again in search of a mate.

Q Do spiders ever get caught in their own webs?

—Jim Mann, Ames, Iowa

A They do, in fact, but they're pretty good at extricating themselves. Unlike their prey, they don't deepen their entanglement by panicking, and it's suspected that they might spit web-dissolving enzymes. Then too, their hard, chitinous claws are snag resistant, unlike, say, the scales on a moth's wings or the setae on a fly's legs. Mind you, not all spider silk is sticky. Some spiders have different glands for different types of silk; only the patient mastermind behind the intricate cobweb knows which of its strands are tacky and which aren't. Weavers of orb webs restrict their perambulations to the radii, which are always smooth. And because the stickum comes not uniformly but in the form of tiny, discrete beads, most spiders can negotiate even their gummiest strands, deftly tiptoeing among the droplets of doom.

Q How do monarch butterflies stay on course while migrating between Mexico and the United States?

—J. Espy, Lima, Ohio

A Like most migrating species, butterflies use internal "compasses" to monitor the sun's position and maintain their headings during the annual eight hundred-mile migration. But there's more: Monarchs home in on the chemical odor of billions of fallen butterfly scales at lepidoptera-friendly rest stops en route and use traces of magnetite in their wings to detect magnetic charges in the rocks. Superb pilotage notwithstanding, the flight does have inherent dangers. Stout winds dash some errant fliers to the ground, whereas others die of exhaustion and starvation during the four-week trek. "But you've got to give their tiny brains credit," says Thomas C. Emmel, professor of entomology and zoology at University of Florida, Gainesville. "It's a remarkable journey."

Q In late summer and fall, why do so many bugs end up dead on their backs, with their feet in the air?

—Mark Baker, Goleta, California

A Bugs are out there dying all the time, of course, all summer long. But when the first cold snap comes, they start dying in exponentially greater numbers. Insects, being cold-blooded creatures, whose body heat closely mirrors the outside temperature, generally start shutting down below fifty degrees Fahrenheit. They thump about, but their hearts aren't in it anymore. A hard freeze and they're goners. As for how bugs lie in state: Because their legs are light and spindly, most bugs are top-heavy. If they die in a tree or on the wing, they tend to land heavy side down, not unlike a slice of toast loaded with jam. Even when one expires right side up, the wind will blow its carcass around until it ends up as gravity prefers: flat on its back. A sadder scenario involves those ill-fated bugs, especially certain beetles, that get flipped on their back and can't right themselves. Luckily, many bugs can wave their legs or flex their wing covers until they're right side up again. The click beetle can simply spring into the air; the firefly uses its bendable thorax to perform a somersault, postponing (for now) the bottoms-up fate of its many Volkswagen-shaped peers.

How come there are a jillion
worms in the morning on streets
and sidewalks after a big
rainstorm? What becomes of
them?

—Ken Younger, Bozeman, Montana

A Yes, this is a grave and woeful occurrence that constantly thins out the ranks of the annelid world. At
nighttime after a good rain shower, worms by the thousands will emerge from their burrows and other hiding
places, stimulated by changes in barometric pressure and
enticed by the moist conditions on the surface. Because
their bodies are more than 80 percent water with highly
permeable skin, they can venture out into the open air
only when it's both dark and extremely humid outside;
it's the only time they can play around on the surface
without shriveling up. An evening shower, therefore, is an
occasion of great excitement for red wigglers, night
crawlers, and the rest of their kind. They freely rove
about, making easy loops over the wet topsoil and stuff-
ing themselves with newly softened organic matter. But
then something horrible happens: the sun comes up. A
worm can abide no more than ten minutes of direct sunlight. Those unlucky revelers that have strayed from the
grass onto pavement are thus caught out in the open, and
because they have no eyes, they can't see the way back to
the grass, even if it's just a few short feet away. The ultra-
violet rays literally paralyze them, and they start to dry
out. By midmorning, you have a worm apocalypse on

your hands, with hundreds dead and dying, and the last survivors wriggling helplessly on a battlefield of concrete, impaled by the sun. Cars squish them. Skateboards roll over them. And for the early bird, it's an all-you-can-eat smorgasbord.

Q As a kid growing up in South America, I'd capture ants and put them to my ear. I could hear them screaming! Was I hallucinating?

—Carlos Dell Acqua, Los Angeles, California

A Don't worry, you heard something. And you don't have to go all the way back to South America to hear it again. The renowned evolutionary biologist and ant authority Edward O. Wilson calls it "the interesting music of the ants." It's a form of stridulation, a sound created by rubbing two body parts together—the same kind of thing crickets do. Many ants, including the leaf-cutter ant that is so abundant in South America, have a washboard affair on their rear end. They scrape the washboard with a "plectrum," producing an audible squeak that serves to warn of danger or to recruit new grunts in their various public works projects. In your neck of the woods, Wilson suggests listening to red harvester ants, which are common in the western and southern United States and make nests that look like little craters surrounded by pebbles. But be careful when you pick them up: Their bite is worse than their squeak.

Q Why do fireflies light up?

—Collin Warner, Atlanta, Georgia

A Fireflies live most of their short lives as larvae, eating like fiends in order to build up energy for sex. Come summertime, the larvae transform into the blinking, winged beetles we know so well. But their days are numbered (to about seven, in fact), so they spend nearly every minute engaged in a frantic hunt for a mate. Which is where those little bursts of bioluminescence—caused by a complex chemical reaction involving an enzyme known as *luciferase*—come in. "It's the way male lightning bugs advertise their services," explains University of Florida entomologist James E. Lloyd, noting that each species has its own signature style, composed of complicated variations of flickers and pulses. When the waiting female, hunkered safely in the grass or atop a branch, lays her tiny beetle eyes on a particularly enticing sexual semaphore, she flashes a slow, seductive come-hither signal and mating begins—a feat that can take hours. Could there be a more compelling reason to free them from their mason jars?

Q In March the snow fleas appear in New England. What are they? What do they eat?

—J. Lumbard, Hollis, New Hampshire

A Snow fleas are insects, but they aren't really fleas. They belong to the order Collembola, the springtails, whose name derives from an odd-looking forked appendage tucked under the body that allows them to hop around. Springtails are amazingly common, with something like 3,500 species found everywhere from pole to pole, living in soil, in leaf litter, and on the surface of water, as well as on snow. And they're around pretty much all the time; it's just that their dark bodies are more conspicuous against a white background.

Unlike real fleas, snow fleas don't feed on blood and thus do not bite people (or dogs). They subsist on wind-carried pollen, fungi, spider dung, dust particles, and certain forms of algae that grow on the surface of snow. Uncanny survivors, they produce an antifreeze-like compound that prevents their body cells from rupturing in extreme cold.

By the way, snow fleas aren't the only creepy-crawlies lurking in your snow: There are also winter stone flies, spiders, ice worms—on and on it goes. So next time you're tempted to scoop up a thirst-quenching mouthful of "virgin" powder, think twice.

Q Most ticks are deaf, blind, and slow as Christmas. So how do they find you?

—Melissa Shepherd, Lincoln, Nebraska

A They smell you. Scientists have learned what sets ticks off by attaching itty-bitty electrodes to the olfactory organs on their legs. At a range of about twenty or thirty feet, a tick can smell the carbon dioxide on your breath. Closer in—a few feet away—it begins to respond to ammonia and other chemicals in your sweat, and closer still, it becomes stimulated by your body heat. Basically, there are two kinds of ticks: "Ambush" ticks sit patiently on vegetation, waiting with their forelegs extended, until a likely critter brushes against them. "Hunter" ticks, on the other hand, will actually go after their prey, engaging in hot pursuits of thirty feet or more. And they're faster than you might think. Daniel Sonenshine, author of *The Biology of the Tick*, has clocked a tick crossing his desk in less than ten seconds. Impressive, yes. But consider that only one tick in a million finds enough food to survive to adulthood. Nature is inefficient, thank goodness.

Q Can bees really detect fear in humans?

—*Bill McCracken, Cheyenne, Wyoming*

A As far as we know, bees and wasps are not psychics. When a group of hikers comes dumbly clomping through their territory, bees have no telepathic knack for singling out the one bee-o-phobe hiding among the stoics. And yet the bee-o-phobe is indeed the one who often gets stung. Why is this? It just so happens that many of the typical manifestations of human fear are exactly the things that make bees more aggressive. Like many insects, bees don't have exceptionally sharp vision, so they've evolved other senses to detect threats to the queen and her hive. For starters, they're expert at detecting motion. And if there is one kind of motion that they hate, it's sudden, jerky motion—exactly the sort of erratic flailing people exhibit when they panic. (Hence the tai chi fluidity of professional beekeepers.) A panicked person also tends to hyperventilate and to sweat—two more traits that can set bees on edge, as they are extraordinarily sensitive to sudden chemical changes in our sweat and breath. "If you're frightened, you exhale more CO_2, and the odors of your sweat become more pungent," notes USDA research entomologist Justin Schmidt. "Bees are one thousand times more sensitive to certain chemicals than we are." If you're venturing into African killer bee country, do what Schmidt does: wear light-colored, long-sleeve clothing, move very s-l-o-w-l-y, and—no kidding—hold your breath. After you get stung once, however, panic does become a prudent response, Schmidt says, because the first bee that nails you plants a pheromone on your body that acts as a homing device for all its stinging compatriots. You're marked. "In that case," says Schmidt, "what you want to do is channel all of your panic to your legs—and make a fast exit."

Q If sweaters get moths, do sheep?
—Beth Austin, Oak Park, Illinois

A Not to be a stickler, but the moths themselves actually aren't the issue. The adult webbing clothes moth, as the pest is properly known, has no functional mouth and thus cannot bore holes in your favorite mohair or the fleece of an innocent lamb. Only the larvae eat. And as it happens, moth larvae are a bit . . . *sheepish,* fearful of light and movement. For this reason, your average ewe grazing out in a sunlit pasture somewhere won't be nibbled. A sack of sheared fleece, on the other hand, would be in peril, as would, say, a really lethargic sheep living in a pitch-black barn.

By the way, moth larvae dine not only on wool, but on anything containing *keratin,* the basic protein in animal fibers. "They survive in dead birds and other carcasses in protected places," explains entomologist Thomas Allen Parker, who edited the chapter on moths in the definitive *Handbook of Pest Control.* "If you have a pigeon problem in your attic, you'll have a moth problem in the rest of your house."

Q I remember, as a lad, counting cricket chirps to come up with the temperature, but I've forgotten the formula. Can you help?
—*Dan Boles, Revelstoke, British Columbia, Canada*

A Count the chirps over a thirteen-second period and add forty. That'll give the temperature in degrees Fahrenheit, give or take a bit. The only trick is that the formula works for just one species: the snowy tree cricket, *Oecanthus fultoni.* Luckily, though, snowy tree crickets are found throughout most of North America. To find them, go out in the evening, starting in mid-July, and listen for what University of Florida entomologist Tom Walker calls "a low-pitched melodious chirp" such as you might hear in night scenes on TV westerns. Walker should know: He named the species back in the 1960s. "All crickets are pretty good thermometers," Walker explains. "They rub their wings at a rate directly proportional to the temperature." It's just that snowy tree crickets are more accurate than most; their chirps are slow enough to be counted, and they synchronize their fiddling, so you don't have to struggle to pick out a pattern from the surrounding din. Nature goes to a lot of trouble so you can amaze your friends. Be grateful.

piscine pondering

Q What makes fish "fishy"?

—Bertram Thule Jr., London, England

A The sensory experts will tell you that, technically speaking, you can't *taste* "fishy," you can only smell it. But in fact taste is so intimately linked with olfaction that this is almost a semantic distinction. The fishy taste is like pornography—hard to define, but we instantly know it when we encounter it. When fish flesh ages, and its fatty oils become exposed to oxygen, certain compounds are manufactured. These compounds—the most common ones are known as *amines* and *unsaturated aldehydes*—are what cause insult to our noses and taste buds.

"To be blunt," says Richard Rosenblatt, a marine biologist at the Scripps Institution of Oceanography, "it's the reek of fish oil going rancid." It doesn't necessarily mean that the whole fish is spoiled, just that its oils are fast becoming oxidized. Generally speaking, the oilier and fattier the fish, the more rapidly it develops the offending odor. Tuna and salmon, for example, can get ripe in a hurry.

Now, there's a second class of stench/taste that we commonly associate with fish, particularly freshwater fish that swim around in slightly muddy water full of slimy vegetation. If you take a dip in a river or lake, you can often detect it in the water—a kind of mildewy, time-to-clean-out-the-aquarium smell. Basically, it's the smell of algae, living and dead, but anything swimming in the water will begin to take on its distinctive redolence. So if your Cajun catfish is fresh but still somehow tastes vaguely fishy, it's probably not the meat, it's the medium.

Q What is "lake turnover" and what's it do to the fish?

—Franklin Genovese, Dallas, Texas

A Along with the more overt signs of fall's arrival— geese winging south, pumpkins swelling on the vine, hordes of Winnebagos spoiling the Vermont foliage— comes an almost imperceptible telltale of the season: lake turnover, or *inversion,* as it's known among snooty limnologists. Almost all bodies of freshwater and some saline lakes turn over every autumn. Here's how it works: Ordi-

Piscine pondering
191

narily lakes are stratified into well-defined thermal bands; the deeper you go, the more frigid the waters. But as the mercury drops in the fall, the lake's warmer, lighter, more oxygenated surface water cools and settles. Aided by the wind, the different layers get mixed up, so that the lake becomes nearly uniform in temperature and oxygen content from top to bottom. In this confusing world, fish often stop feeding (turnover season is renowned as the time when anglers reacquaint themselves with their families). In extreme cases, turnover can churn up enough oxygen-deficient water to cause dramatic fish kills. Some lakes develop a murky green hue and an odd stench, the smell of rotting organic matter that's been stirred up. But it's all fleeting. Come winter, ice forms on the surface, the wind ceases to be a player, and stratification again sets up shop.

Q Why do flying fish fly?

—Michael C. Rusch, San Clemente, California

A All forty or so species of tropical flying fish have oversize pectoral fins that when extended serve as airfoils. Unlike birds, they don't flap. Whooshing toward the ocean surface, flying fish beat their tails until they reach takeoff velocities of between twenty and forty miles per hour, outstripping some speedboats. They then launch themselves as much as sixty feet—to the great consternation of boaters nearby. Wayward Redwings, one of the most common species of flying fish, routinely smack into sailors; in one probably apocryphal story, a flying fish is reported to have whacked a woman so hard that she perished. More commonly they just startle cruise-line passengers and become the stuff of great UFO fish tales.

But why fly at all? "If you throw yourself out of the water, you get out of a predator's sight," says University of West Chester biologist Frank Fish (really), who has a sweetly empathic habit of referring to fish in the second person. "Since you control the flight path, you can curve off or decide when you drop back into the water."

Unless, of course, there happens to be yet another predator stationed nearby with a net in hand: some flying fish are edible and highly sought after by fishermen.

Q When lightning hits water, how come the fish aren't electrocuted?

—J. T. Stanton, Princeton, New Jersey

A They *are* electrocuted. You're just too busy scrambling from the water to see it. As lightning expert Martin A. Uman puts it, when a bolt strikes a river or lake, all the fish within a few yards "come up dead, their little mouths pointing toward the sky as if in prayer."

Fish don't seem to have any special tolerance for high voltage. "Electric eels kill their fish prey by shocking them," notes Uman. "Some people even go fishing that way. They'll put high voltage things in the water and just scoop 'em up."

Q Why are saltwater fish unable to survive in freshwater, and vice versa?

—Jason Brewer, Waddy, Kentucky

A The underlying science can be a little complicated—involving divalent ions and osmotic gradients and other unspeakable torments from advanced chemistry class—but the crux of the problem lies deep in the piscine kidney. Because their kidneys are designed to retain as much water as possible, saltwater fish pass a highly concentrated form of urine that's thick and viscous and loaded up with the excess salts that their bodies are constantly taking in through the gills and mouth. If a flounder were to venture into a river or lake, it would quickly swell up and die (and possibly burst) from fluid retention, as its miserly kidneys would be unable to pass the strangely thin urine quickly enough. A freshwater fish has exactly the opposite problem. Should a brown trout blunder into the Atlantic, it would quickly shrivel up and expire from acute dehydration, not unlike a slug seasoned with a pinch of Morton's; its kidneys, designed to excrete an extremely dilute urine, would dump too much precious H_2O too fast. Of course, there are anadromous species such as steelhead and salmon that can go both ways, but before a salmon smolt can head into the open sea, it spends a week or so acclimatizing in the brackish water of an estuary, its thyroid gland and gills undergoing a metamorphosis that enables it to withstand the ocean's high salt concentrations—thirty-three parts per thousand.

further life forms

"All those salts are trying to suck the water out of a fish's body," explains marine biologist Richard Rosenblatt of the Scripps Institution of Oceanography. "Throw a freshwater fish into the sea and it's like putting a jungle orchid in the Sahara."

green genes

Good dirt from the plant world

Q I've heard that kissing under mistletoe was a pagan fertility rite long before it became a Christmas tradition. Is this true?

—Lars Smitts, Tempe, Arizona

A People have believed in the special powers of mistletoe, *Viscum album*, since the Bronze Age. Druids thought the plant was heaven sent, perhaps because it seems to appear out of nowhere: It's a parasite that taps its rootlike "sinkers" into a host tree and literally sucks the life juices out of it. It grows slowly, ruthlessly, and doesn't die until its host dies. At the winter solstice, a white-robed Druid priest would climb an oak and use a golden sickle to harvest mistletoe, which most ancient Europeans considered a cure-all, good for toothache, epilepsy, and yes, infertility. (Today we know that mistletoe is poisonous, though researchers recently found that a leaf extract might inhibit the growth of cancer cells and bolster the immune system.) In ancient Rome, the plant was regarded as a symbol of peace. Enemies would discard their weapons under a sprig, declare a truce, and embrace. It was in Victorian England, however, that smooching under mistletoe became fashionable as a romantic Yuletide tradition—and it continues today as the one occasion each year when Brits actually touch.

Q What kinds of trees absorb the most carbon dioxide?

—Aaron Agontar, Coconut Creek, Florida

A All green plants absorb carbon dioxide from the atmosphere through their leaves during photosynthesis, but the amount fluctuates greatly. Carbon dioxide absorption falls off during the winter when deciduous trees lose their leaves, and it skyrockets when buds reemerge in early spring. Older trees plagued by deteriorating cells, as well as those rooted in colder climes, grow slowly and thus absorb less carbon dioxide, consuming an average of about five pounds a year, whereas the fastest-sprouting trees with a year-round growing season inhale the most. How much? Rainforest trees such as members of the genus *Leucaena,* which typically grow from seed to twenty-foot-tall saplings in their first year, absorb about fifty pounds annually—roughly the amount of exhaust one car spews out in an hour. Says EPA ecologist Sandra Brown of the University of Illinois: "It's not what you'd call an encouraging ratio."

Q How exactly does poison ivy wreak its havoc?

—Pauline Harris, Seattle, Washington

A Poison ivy wouldn't be poisonous without a certain oily sap known as *urushiol,* which lurks in almost every part of the plant. Contact with as little as one-millionth of a gram can trigger the chain of dermatological reactions that leads to the usual blistery, suppurating mess. Urushiol is an evil, evil thing. An extremely stable compound, it's been found, in an active state, in desiccated plants more than one hundred years old. It sticks around in dead vines, it clings to dogs that you pet and shoelaces that you tie, it lingers on gardening tools that you neglect to rinse with isopropyl alcohol. Burn poison ivy and the oil will go airborne, where it can torture you with unspeakable, unreachable itchiness in your lungs and trachea. Of all animals, only we humans seem to suffer poison ivy's epidermal ravages: Some birds eat its berries, rodents nest among its leaves, bears sleep on it. Urushiol appears to have been created merely to make humans miserable—while giving calamine merchants a purpose in life.

Q Why aren't acorns just called oak nuts?

—Margaret Byrd, Mobile, Alabama

A *Acorn* was originally a generic term for all the varieties of nuts that accumulate on the forest floor each fall. In Chaucer's day, if you wanted to be specific, you'd have to say "acorns of oak."

Acorn comes from the same family of words as *acre.* However, it just so happens that the Old English word for *oak* is *ac.* Because of this phonetic similarity, people in the British Isles began to make the not unreasonable assumption that acorns must specifically be the seeds—*corns,* in Old English—of ac trees, and by the sixteenth century the original meaning of the word had been lost.

There's no end to linguistic evolution, of course. In parts of the United States today, in fact, people call oaks "acorn trees"—a construction that puts the chicken before the egg, but at least it's consistent.

Q Why do weeping willows weep?

—Cliff Paige, Frankfort, Kentucky

A Originally a native of China, the weeping willow, *Salix babylonica,* has traveled widely and hybridized promiscuously. The tree's exaggerated droop has made it a metaphor for sorrow at least since biblical times. ("By the rivers of Babylon . . . we wept . . . [and] hanged our harps upon the willows . . ." Psalms 137.) Claude

Monet, himself a prodigious planter of willows, painted a famous series of the weepers in 1919 after the French signed the Armistice Treaty to symbolize a nation in mourning.

But why the hangdog expression? "They're depressed?" suggests Frank Santamore, eminent tree physiologist at National Arboretum, before offering a confession of abject ignorance: "Actually, we don't know for sure. It's just never been studied at the cellular level."

Some botanists have speculated that the tree's familiar wilt might have something to do with a geotropic response gone awry (and who are we to dispute them?). A far more compelling theory, however, suggests that the name derives from the fact that so many willows have been known to make their *owners* weep. Willows might look harmless as they sway lugubriously in a gentle breeze, but beneath the ground they're all business. Under no circumstances should you ever plant one near your house. "Their roots are very fibrous and extremely aggressive," says Dr. Nick Gawel, a plant DNA expert at the Tennessee State University Nursery Crop Research Station. "They wrap their roots around everything. They can ruin your septic system and even your house foundation. They're a disaster!"

It is perhaps telling that the willow doesn't weep until it reaches maturity. "It will grow upright for a certain number of years," says Gawel, "and then later in life it starts to bend over—rather like the rest of us."

Q Why can't we get syrup from trees other than maples? Is oaken pancake syrup possible?

—Nick Galbreath, Boston, Massachusetts

A You can make syrup from the sap of many other trees, such as the butternut and the box elder, a cousin of the maple. There's even minor commercial production of birch syrup. But for the most part, only the sugar maple is blessed with a variety of sap that's sweet enough to make its harvest worthwhile. You'd have to boil down 150 gallons of birch sap to render a single gallon of syrup; with maple sap, the ratio is about forty to one.

Sweetness, however, is just part of the story. Most trees don't "bleed" sap like maples do. (Even maples bleed significantly only in late winter and early spring, as they prepare to emerge from dormancy.) Oaks have a more evolved circulatory system. They transport fluids only in a narrow ring under the bark, so they heal quickly when cut.

Even if you could collect a bucket of oak squeezins, you might not want them center stage on your flapjacks. According to U.S. Forest Service plant pathologist Phil Wargo, "Ring-porous trees like oaks convert carbohydrates into brown grungy things." The grunge helps fight off fungi, which are big killers of trees. Very useful for the oak, of course, but not terribly appetizing.

Q What was the biggest pumpkin ever grown?

—*Sam Breuer, Redwood City, California*

A In 1998, Gary Burke of Simcoe, Ontario, left pumpkin fans agog with a monster that weighed in at 1,092 pounds. Most world records have come from the northern United States and Canada, along the 45th parallel. (Stray south of that and you get into humongous watermelon territory, which is a whole different story.) Competitors let their vines sprawl out as much as 1,500 square feet, and they pile on some ten cubic yards of composted manure per plant. Former record holder Herman Bax, of Brockville, Ontario, is rumored to have placed his patch directly over an old septic field (he's not talking). During the peak season, in midsummer, a world-class pumpkin will slurp up more than one thousand gallons of water per week and take on thirty pounds per day. Sometimes they grow so fast that they explode.

Elite pumpkin growers are as serious about genealogy as Kentucky Thoroughbred breeders. Most of the champs are descended from a line known as Howard Dill's Atlantic Giant. A seed scraped from a world champion can fetch $10, and as some of these monstrosities hold as many as seven hundred seeds, some growers have made a nice cottage industry out of pumpkin husbandry. But most people simply do it for the thrill. Reminiscing on her 968-pound leviathan from 1995, champion grower Paula Zehr of Lowville, New York, says, "We were just very excited to see something that could get that big."

Q I should know this, but what's the difference between a fruit and a vegetable?

—Ed Miller, Putney, Vermont

A At the risk of descending into gratuitous prurience, a fruit is any soft, swollen plant flesh—or "ovary"—embedded with seeds. Fruits are the products of pollinated flowers growing on trees, bushes, and perennial vines. Because they're naturally designed to be carried away and ravished by animals like us so as to disperse the seeds, fruits are often bright, sweet tasting, or otherwise enticing in aspect. The definition of a vegetable is murkier. Generally, a vegetable plant is considered any annual growth that yields edible food (excluding grains, which for some reason we've always lumped into a special category). In our imprecise slang, we tend to call the produce of any vegetable plant "a vegetable," but botanists prefer to talk about the specific anatomical parts that we are consuming, such as leaves (spinach), roots (carrots), shoots (asparagus), flowers (broccoli), and so on. Unfortunately, some so-called veggies—such as peppers, squash, cucumbers, eggplant, and pumpkins—are fleshy, seed-stuffed products of pollinated flowers. In other words, they're fruits, even though we mulishly persist in calling them otherwise. This brings us to the tomato, arguably the most misunderstood foodstuff of all. By every reasonable definition, it's a fruit, though not according to an 1893 Supreme Court decision that declared it a vegetable. (There was a trade war going on, and imported veggies were subject to tariff.) Now, more than a century later, the confusion still lingers and is bound to deepen, as mad geneticists at Monsanto and Upjohn concoct a futuristic crop of Frankenfoods, further blurring an already blurry line.

Q Why does moss grow on rocks? What's the appeal?

—Carl Stokes, Storrs, Connecticut

A In a word, stability. It's an anchorage affording some measure of stasis in a turbulent world. Though a moss plant (or lichen) doesn't need its rock for daily food and drink in the way that a tree needs its soil, without *something* to attach to, these swatches of green velvet would be nothing more than common vagrants, consigned to tumble in the wind until they shriveled and died. So a long time ago the mosses decided to hitch their fate to stationary things—tree roots, cathedral walls, and especially (how can you beat them, really?) rocks. Moss plants have hundreds of sticky root hairs called *rhyzoids*—lichens, on the other hand, have little clasping tentacles called *hyphae*—with which they grab onto the rock surface and don't let go. Over time, the acidic compounds in the plants themselves will slowly digest the rock surface, allowing them an even firmer purchase on their real estate. This dissolved crust, in turn, provides the moss and lichen with a bit of calcium and other trace minerals that help their body grow twelve ways. Moss and lichen can be extremely finicky about their choice of rock. Some species will only glom onto limestone, others only basalt or coarse granite. Light exposure, pH, porousness, proximity to water drainage—each species of moss and lichen has a different set of requirements. Once they find a suitable stone and set up housekeeping, where do they get the primary sustenance to go on living? "You'd be surprised," says Alan Whittemore, a noted *bryologist,* or moss expert, at the Missouri Botanical Garden. "They can get food from wind-blown dirt, from dead leaves that land on them, from nutrients suspended in water that drips from overhanging trees. Even a rat that comes along every twenty years and leaves a single dropping can provide a significant source of nourishment." *Bon appétit.*

Q What is foxfire, and how do I find it?

—Steven M. Yates, Sugar Land, Texas

A There are subjects you stumble on from time to time that sort of unnerve and mystify the hard scientists. Foxfire is one of them. Not that there's any doubt about its existence; it's just that foxfire, sometimes known as *faerie fire* or *cold fire* or *will-o'-the-wisp,* is a phenomenon that borders on the magical, and unless you know exactly what you're looking for, it can be virtually impossible to find. Simply put, foxfire is a blue-green luminescence caused by the fibrous roots of microscopic fungi that grow inside extremely rotten timber. It's the faint electricity of decay, the slow smolder of mushrooms digesting cellulose.

Written accounts of foxfire date at least as far back as fifteenth-century England, but the scientific literature on it is scant. We called half a dozen of the nation's preeminent tree experts, and they didn't know a thing about it. Then we tracked down the man who must surely be the world authority on the subject, at least from the standpoint of hands-on experience. Clyde Hollifield is a welder who lives in Bunkum County, in the mountains of North Carolina. He's a self-taught naturalist who has published articles on foxfire; clearly he's a man who's clocked some serious quality time in the deep woods. To find foxfire, says Hollifield, you need to have a warm, moonless, pitch-black night. Not just any woods will do; you need what Hollifield calls "old, damp, rotten, manky woods, and preferably a real diverse stand" (not a monoculture). Hunt around on the forest floor for soppy wet stumps and logs. Fast-rotting blond woods like poplar, beech, and birch are best. Then look for the telltale signs of fungal infestation: bark that's streaked and splotchy and studded with the caps of soft gill mushrooms. Sometimes you'll see the glow right away, but usually you'll have to take these chunks of rotten wood and disturb them, crumble them up, get the inner tissues exposed to the air. Then, a few hours later, the light show begins. "Once you get it glowing," says Hollifield, "it's not at all subtle. It's a bright elfin green.

You can see it glowing through a brown paper bag. You can throw it in a creek and it'll look like emeralds floating downstream—water won't put it out. You can write your name with it on the ground. It's fun to mess with." This bioluminescence, Hollifield believes, is the result of a complex chemical reaction that's set off when the tiny fibrous roots of certain fungi are exposed to the air, a reaction that involves "the real complicated alkaloids of mushrooms deep in the digestion process."

Once you've found a trove of foxfire, don't get too attached to it: It's ephemeral stuff. "That glow is the tree's finale, its last gasp," says Hollifield. "It may have been waiting thirty years getting ready for this one night, but it will only glow once. And then it's gone forever."

index